WHAT'S THE POINT OF THEOLOGY?

Wisdom, wellbeing and wonder

Alister McGrath

What's the Point of Theology

First published in Great Britain in 2022

Society for Promoting Christian Knowledge
36 Causton Street
London SW1P 4ST
www.spck.org.uk

ISBN 978-0-310-15190-6 (softcover)
ISBN 978-0-310-15208-8 (audio)
ISBN 978-0-310-15206-4 (ebook)

British Library Cataloguing-in-Publication Data
A catalogue record for this book is available from the British Library

ISBN 978-0-281-08689-4
eBook ISBN 978-0-281-08690-0

Typeset by Manila Typesetting Company
First printed in Great Britain by Ashford Colour Press

Printed in the United States of America

22 23 24 25 26 27 28 29 30 31 32 /TRM/ 15 14 13 12 11 10 9 8 7 6 5 4 3 2 1

Contents

Part 2
WHY THEOLOGY MATTERS: WISDOM, WELLBEING AND WONDER

Introduction

I had never heard of theology when I discovered Christianity as an undergraduate at the University of Oxford back in 1971. All that changed three years later as I was reading C. S. Lewis's essay 'Is theology poetry?'[1] Lewis (1898–1963) gave me a fleeting glimpse of something tantalizingly distant yet eminently desirable, like a shimmering Tuscan landscape. I experienced a sense of wonder as I pondered his elegant prose, feeling that I was being drawn into a world beyond any I knew.

Yet most of my Christian friends at Oxford at the time saw theology as pointless speculation irrelevant to the life of faith. Others, particularly those studying philosophy, argued that theology was simply meaningless. They'd read A. J. Ayer's *Language, Truth and Logic* (1936), and believed that it justified their secular common-sense rationalism. Ayer set out a 'principle of verification', which asserted that a statement is meaningful only if it can be verified. Since Ayer (1910–89) held the Wykeham Chair of Logic at the University of Oxford throughout my years as an undergraduate, it was no surprise that his ideas dominated student philosophical debate. Theology, it seemed, was doomed to an inevitable intellectual extinction.

My decision to switch from the natural sciences to theology in the mid-1970s thus seemed unwise, perhaps even mad, to most of my Oxford friends. But that was fifty years ago and things have moved on. Ayer's 'principle of verification' is now seen as unworkable and self-contradictory. As the atheist philosopher Julian Baggini (b. 1968) points out, Ayers's discredited views are now echoed mainly in the simplistic and superficial certainties of New Atheist writers such as Richard Dawkins (b. 1941), who urge us to forget about God, stop worrying and instead just enjoy life.[2]

Dawkins's assurance that science can answer all of life's questions has lost its initial credibility, now being seen as an exercise in intellectual circularity presupposing its own conclusions in order to confirm them. Most people now prefer to keep an open mind on the matter, having a vague sense that there might be 'something there' and wondering what more religious souls think.

I hope this short book will be helpful to those of you who are curious and puzzled about theology, perhaps struggling to understand the apparent confidence with which it speaks about things you consider to be tentative and uncertain. I hope it will also engage readers who attend church yet feel suspicious and sceptical about the subject. Let me be clear: many intelligent and reflective people, both religious and secular, have deep misgivings about theology! Is it pointless nonsense, like debating how many angels can dance on a pinhead? Is it a distraction from more important aspects of faith, such as the beauty of worship, the joy of praise and the satisfaction of serving our communities? Why is it expressed in such inaccessible technical vocabulary, so far from the simple yet rich language of the New Testament?

As I come to the end of my career as a professor of theology at the University of Oxford, I would like to share something of what I've learned. I may be wrong in some of my judgements! But the concerns expressed above (and others) will be taken seriously as I explore what theology is really all about – why it remains important for those inside and beyond the community of faith, the difference it can make to the ways in which Christians think and live, and how it fits into the wider human quest for wisdom, wellbeing and wonder.

Alister McGrath

Part 1

THEOLOGY: SOME OPENING REFLECTIONS

1

Discovering theology: seeing things in a new way

Theology is pointless. It doesn't do anything useful. Practical ministry is what really matters. Why waste time teaching future Christian leaders about theology when they could instead feast on the latest theories of church growth, congregational management and counselling skills?

As I know from many conversations, these views are widespread in denominational bureaucracies. I think they are understandable, though I can't help feeling that they've not been properly thought through. Nobody wants to devote time and resources to doing something pointless. But what if theology sustains the vision that lies at the heart of the Christian faith? What if theology has a unique and necessary role to play in keeping this vision alive and thus energizing and sustaining the life, worship and outreach of the Church?

Such questions are relevant not only to Christianity but also to any group, institution or organization with a strong sense of identity and mission. How can we maintain continuity with the past while making sure that we connect up with today's issues? Some organizations die because what initially inspired them has become irrelevant. But more often, they fade away because they have lost sight of their founding vision and can't work out how to recover and refresh it.

Churches that fail to take theology seriously risk turning their backs on a rich and invaluable heritage and diminishing their capacity to engage the hearts and captivate the imaginations of a new generation. I'll be exploring these themes throughout this book, drawing on leading theologians from the past and present to argue that theology is essential to the life, ministry and witness of the Christian churches, and to their engagement with wider culture.

Let's focus here on why theology matters for individuals and for churches. I've suggested that it sets out the vision which lies at the heart of the Christian faith and underlies the worship and life of Christian communities. Theology unpacks the core themes of faith. It tells us how these were developed, illustrates how they may be explained and preached and shows us the difference they make to real life. Above all, theology sets out the Christian understanding of how we can achieve wisdom, enjoy wellbeing and nurture a sense of wonder.

The Christian gospel is like a watering hole in the midst of a desert that attracts people because it offers something Christians believe is both liberating and essential. Christ's words to the Samaritan woman when they met at Jacob's well illustrate this point perfectly:

> Everyone who drinks this water will be thirsty again, but whoever drinks the water I give them will never thirst. Indeed, the water I give them will become in them a spring of water welling up to eternal life.
> (John 4.13–14)

Theology sustains and expresses this understanding of what a fulfilled life looks like and how it comes about through the person and work of Christ.

Theology thus captures and puts into words the moral, intellectual and spiritual vision that is the heartbeat of the Christian faith – a way of seeing things that delights and overwhelms us and leads to worship and adoration rather than mere understanding. It wrestles with the question of how Christians can hope to express this defining and compelling vision in words. It helps us to explain what Christianity is fundamentally *about* and enables us to convey the difference that such an understanding makes to the way in which we comprehend our world and live within it. Theology helps preachers to open up the riches of the Christian faith and apologists to explain and defend its leading themes to a wider culture.

It's important that people outside the Christian community get a sense of theology's driving and empowering vision even if they don't share it. I used to be a Marxist. While I've left Marxism behind, I still have a good appreciation of its world view and implications. I no longer think that it's right, but I can see why it's important. You don't need to agree with something to understand it, and understanding it will mean that you're more clued up about how people try to make sense of our complicated world.

Institutions, including churches, must continually ask themselves these questions: why are we here? What sparked us into existence and empowers us today? In his important study of how institutional visions are developed, articulated and put into practice, Daniel Pekarsky emphasizes the importance of a 'well-conceived vision', which he defines as 'an informing idea that is shared, clear and compelling.'[1] Such visions can easily go out of date due to social and cultural change. Christianity, however, rests on a *theological* vision statement focusing on God and humanity: on the one hand, we have a loving and personal God who journeys with us through life; on the other, a broken, wounded and damaged humanity in need of love, restoration and hope.

These themes must be articulated in a meaningful way for each new generation. We do not need to *make* Christianity relevant, but the task of both theologian and preacher is to unpack and unfold the riches of this vision of faith using language, images, stories and concepts that connect with our audience.

There is always a hermeneutical (interpretative) element to a vision statement, simply because its application will vary from one historical period and cultural location to another. We shall explore this long theological tradition of interpreting the gospel – without compromising its identity – to help us meet new challenges and situations. The Swiss Protestant theologian Emil Brunner (1889–1966) sums things up neatly: 'The gospel remains the same, but our understanding of the gospel must ever be won anew.'[2] Theology both preserves an identity-giving and life-enhancing vision and provides a toolkit for ensuring that churches can engage with the new challenges they face.

For Christians, I would argue, theology is like a treasure chest: it holds the riches of our faith and invites us to reflect on faith's value and purpose. Without theology, Christian churches are simply custodians of memories and habits that might once have been meaningful, but now seem outdated and pointless to outsiders – and to some insiders. Theology allows these memories and habits to be revitalized. It provides a bridge between past and present, allowing the riches of the past to connect with the present and transform it. The Christian gospel may be the same for all times and places but theology, while being rooted in the wisdom of the past, must free itself from the particularities of a bygone age and articulate the good news in new situations.

So where shall we start? Let's begin by thinking about how Christianity enables us to see ourselves, Christ and the world as they truly are. Helpfully, we'll leave behind deficient and inadequate understandings of reality as we embrace a rich, satisfying and transformative vision.

Theology as a new way of seeing things

When I was a teenager, I enjoyed reading the American writer Henry Miller (1891–1980), largely because many of his works explore how the process of travelling changes people by opening their eyes to new realities. A particular line from his colourful depiction of Big Sur on the Californian coastline caught my attention: 'One's destination is never a place, but rather a new way of looking at things.'[3]

Miller's neat one-liner came to mean a lot more to me as I began to study the New Testament closely in the original Greek in January 1972, beginning with the Gospel of Mark. I had only just discovered Christianity and wanted to immerse myself in a text that would help me to understand more about it. I was intrigued by the first words spoken by Christ in Mark's narrative: '"The time has come," he said. "the kingdom of God has come near. Repent and believe the good news!"' (Mark 1.15). The Greek word *metanoia* (usually translated as 'repentance') actually has a much deeper range of meaning that includes, but is not limited to, this single idea. *Metanoia* concerns a change in our mindset leading to a transformed vision.

The world did not change when I moved from atheism to Christianity. *Yet I changed.* Christianity gave me a lens through which everything came into sharper focus and, as a result, I saw the world in a new and very different light. The way I viewed it altered. I then had to work out how I fitted into this new world and how I ought to live on the basis of my new insights. No longer did I see the world as 'nature'; I saw it as God's creation. No longer did I see people as socioeconomic units; I saw them as individuals bearing the image of God.

A good example of viewing things differently is the way in which Christians read the Old Testament. Many of my Jewish colleagues at Oxford see the Hebrew Bible as complete in itself, whereas Christians regard it as preparatory and anticipatory. It points beyond itself for its fulfilment. This is why so many New Testament passages pick up on the way in which the history of Jesus Christ can be said to fulfil Old Testament prophecy, developing its storyline in new ways.

Augustine of Hippo (354–430) summed up this idea thus: 'In the Old Testament the New is concealed, in the New, the Old is revealed.'[4] The point he's making is that the great themes of the New Testament are already there in the Old Testament, but this early text needs to be interpreted or seen in a certain way for these connections and continuities to be appreciated. The New Testament thus provides a Christian lens through which to read the Old Testament, which differs significantly from the lens used by Jewish readers of the same text.

Many theologians have highlighted the capacity of Christian theology to enable us to see things in a new way. A good example is the English poet-theologian George Herbert (1593–1633), who is noted for his ability to express theological ideas in poetic language. Herbert was an academic who served as Orator at the University of Cambridge before spending the final few years of his short life as a country parson in the village of Bemerton, close to the cathedral city of Salisbury.

I often find myself reflecting on the rich theological vision found in Herbert's writings, especially in his poem 'The Elixir'.[5] In its third verse, Herbert offers us two quite distinct ways of doing theology: looking *at* theological ideas and looking *through* them to discover the landscape they disclose:

> A man that looks on glasse,
>   On it may stay his eye;
> Or if he pleaseth, through it passe,
>   And then the heav'n espie.

Herbert's point is easy to grasp. You can look *at* Christian doctrines (for example, the doctrine of creation). That's what I've done throughout my career as an academic theologian. I look *at* this idea, explaining its biblical roots, how it was expressed in the creeds, and how it has been understood by various theologians to my students. Herbert, however, is inviting us to do something additional and rather more interesting. He asks us to look *through* Christian doctrines, to allow Christian theology to become a window to viewing ourselves and the world. He wants us to *use* theology so that we can develop a deeper and richer engagement with our world and see it afresh.

Therefore, instead of merely looking at the doctrine of creation, we ought also to look at our world through the lens provided by this doctrine. Marilynne Robinson (b. 1943), one of the world's most theologically informed contemporary novelists, knows the importance of seeing the natural world properly, for what it really is, through a theological lens: 'Wherever you turn your eyes the world can shine like transfiguration. You don't have to bring a thing to it except a little willingness to see.'[6] We'll return to explore the importance of this theological attentiveness towards the natural order later in the book.

For now, let's work the angles of Herbert's approach to theology. Imagine you are sitting in a room with a single window. You could look *at* the window, noticing only some irritating and distracting specks of dust or smears on the glass. Or you could look *through* the window and take delight in the beautiful garden that lies beyond. Or imagine you are looking at a microscope in a medical laboratory. It's an interesting piece of equipment, but what really matters is that this instrument allows us to examine details of the living world that are completely invisible to the unaided human eye. It extends our vision of reality.

Theology helps us to see things in a new way. However, a habit of engagement is something we need to work at developing. The theologian and psychologist Robert C. Roberts (b. 1942) emphasizes the importance of seeing the world and our experiences in a Christian manner. We must, he suggests, '*practice* seeing things this way. How does one practice seeing? By *looking*. Looking is active seeing, and as we succeed in seeing what we are looking for, we train our seeing into conforming with our looking.'[7] A theologian is someone who cultivates the habit of discernment: seeing things rightly, properly and fully.

Imagining the new world of faith

I've often suggested to my students that it is helpful to think about the Christian faith as a landscape to be explored. How do we find this world? And then enter and explore it? What does it look like? How does it feel to be there?

The answers to these questions are framed in terms of 'faith'. Yet this is not the 'blind faith' so poorly understood – and crudely parodied – by Richard Dawkins. Where Dawkins thinks of faith as a perverse tendency to believe anything we like, Christians see faith as intellectual and relational trust. It involves embracing an expanded vision of reality that enfolds God and enables a transforming relationship. I can't prove that this way of looking at the world is right (although I believe it is), which is a problem I share with Dawkins, who belatedly seems to have realized his atheism is not something that can be proved either. It's a belief, a judgement, a decision to live in a certain way on the basis of what is thought to be true. Dawkins seems to imagine that the Enlightenment marks the watershed when faith was replaced by scientific reason. Yet this new rational outlook was also rooted in faith – a faith that humans were capable of acting rationally and morally without guidance from beyond. As the subsequent fragmentation of rationalism – so deftly depicted by Alasdair MacIntyre (b. 1929) and others – makes clear, the Enlightenment was basically a new ethnocentric faith tradition that tried hard to present itself as standing above history, geography and culture.[8]

Faith is about trusting the Christian view of things and acting appropriately within the new world that it enables us to see and enter. The great social theorist Max Weber (1864–1920) once remarked that rationalism was like an 'iron cage', which imprisons the human spirit.[9] Theology helps us to see that our common-sense rationalism blinds us to what really matters, blocking off certain pathways of exploration that can – and are meant to – lead us to new habits of thinking, experiencing, imagining and living.

The English novelist Evelyn Waugh (1903–66) is best known for his deeply nostalgic novel *Brideshead Revisited* (1945). After his sudden conversion to Catholicism in 1930, Waugh wrote to a friend describing how his new faith allowed him to see things clearly for the first time. Conversion, he wrote, was about stepping out 'into the real world God made; and then begins the delicious process of exploring it limitlessly.'[10] *Brideshead Revisited* was part of Waugh's 'delicious process' of reflection, focusing on the mysterious way in which divine grace shapes and directs individual lives.

In my own case, I abandoned the sinking ship of my teenage atheism and discovered a different way of thinking about things, imagining the world and pursuing the good life – namely, Christianity. It was like being shipwrecked and finding sanctuary on the shoreline of a strange island that gradually disclosed its mysteries and wonder.

It's helpful to think of theology as an intellectual mapping of this world of faith, making connections between its basic themes and exploring how these shape the ways we see things. Paradoxically, Christian theology is a thoroughly practical discipline, aiming for a right understanding that leads naturally into a right lifestyle marked by finding hope in a seemingly hopeless world.

In addition, and very importantly, theology offers a key to unlocking the full significance of some of the greatest works of Western literature – such as Dante's *Divine Comedy*, the novels of Graham Greene or Marilynne Robinson, or the poetry of George Herbert or T. S. Eliot. Yet while theology is certainly helpful for gaining a better understanding of the past and enriching our appreciation of cultural history, it is essential in other ways too.

I've concentrated so far on reassuring individual Christians and churches about the merits of theology. But I need to say more to readers who don't share those convictions. I'm often asked to explain what theology is about to secular audiences and have found C. S. Lewis's idea of a 'supposal' helpful in doing this.[11] Lewis invites his readers to conduct a mental experiment. *Suppose* Christianity is true: what sort of world does it disclose?

This mental experiment involves weaving the basic themes of Christian theology into a 'big picture' and then imagining what it would be like to inhabit such a world. The experiment doesn't require anyone to believe that these ideas are right; it simply invites an act of imaginative empathy – an exercise in exploring perspectives. Aim to think yourself into this world view, explore it from within and try to work out what it feels like to live in this world.

In Lewis's case, this 'supposal' or mental experiment involves telling a story. Suppose that there is a world like Narnia. In the case of our own world, God entered as Jesus Christ. What would happen if God entered into Narnia as a lion? How would that work out? Lewis takes seven volumes to tell us, but his imagination and narrative pace keep us reading, thinking and imagining.

My approach in the second part of this book is to reflect on how a Christian 'big picture' helps us to think about three core themes that are central to meaningful human life: wisdom, wellbeing and wonder. Christian theology has long been concerned with these questions, and we will explore how it is able to stimulate our thinking and what a distinctively Christian understanding of wisdom, wellbeing and wonder might look like.

I hope that this will help readers who are less familiar with Christian beliefs to get a sense of how theology works and the difference that it makes to people. Through an act of *imaginative empathy*, we can step inside this 'big picture' and try to understand how things look and feel within its framework.

Charles Taylor: imagining a new (but real) world

As we seek to imagine the world in a Christian way, it's worth pointing out that theology often makes use of philosophy to help express its ideas and make them accessible to a wider audience. Early Christian theologians, for example, drew on the forms of Platonism that were widespread in late classical antiquity and this allowed them to take part in wider cultural discussions. There were risks in doing this. Some scholars suggest that, in trying to use Platonism to promote Christianity, theologians actually ended up using Christianity to promote Platonism.

However, most theologians consider a dialogue with philosophy to be important and worthwhile. For example, I regularly engage with the British public philosopher Mary Midgley (1919–2018).[12] Why? Because I find her criticism of reductionism and her emphasis on respecting complexity helpful *critically*, in responding to writers such as Richard Dawkins, and *constructively*, in explaining the richness of the Christian faith. I'll return to this point in the following chapter when we look at Midgley's idea of 'mapping' our complicated world.

Theologians have always jostled with philosophers, sometimes critically and sometimes collaboratively. During the thirteenth century, Thomas Aquinas (1225–74) developed a theological approach that drew appreciatively yet critically on Aristotle's philosophy. This allowed him to enter into discussion with Muslims and pagans who would not accept the authority of the Christian Bible (but who liked Aristotle), and also allowed him to develop a philosophically rigorous approach to theology that remains influential in the twenty-first century. This is a good example of a theological engagement with philosophy that enables a wider cultural discussion.

The Canadian philosopher Charles Taylor (b. 1931) has been widely referenced by modern theologians on account of the rigour of his intellectual vision and the quality of his engagement with cultural history. Taylor, who studied philosophy at Oxford during the 1950s, reacted against the inadequacies of the 'logical positivism' of that period, and set out to develop more satisfactory approaches. He came up with the idea of a 'social imaginary', which offers theologians ways of imagining our world, placing ourselves within a 'vision of the larger order' and acting in accordance with this way of seeing things.

For Taylor, a 'social imaginary' is the way in which people 'imagine their social existence, how they fit together with others, how things go on between them and their fellows, the expectations that are normally met, and the deeper normative notions and images that underlie these expectations'.[13] Many theologians find this idea helpful in giving added intellectual substance to their reflections, allowing them to tease out the idea that Christianity offers a new, distinct and trustworthy mode of embracing our world and our lives.

Not everyone, of course, believes that there is such a big picture or grand story to be entered into in this way. Taylor uses the phrase 'neutral self' to describe the detached position of people who do not recognize the existence or authority of any such big pictures. He suggests that those who are unanchored and unattached to any larger vision of reality are 'at sea' when it comes to issues of moral values – questions concerning 'what is good, or worthwhile, or admirable, or of value'. The point Taylor makes is theologically important: we need a 'frame or horizon within which things can take on a stable significance', allowing us to decide what is 'good and meaningful,' or 'bad or trivial'.[14] And for Taylor, theology offers us this kind of 'imaginary': a 'frame or horizon' that helps us make sense of things and live accordingly.

Some would concede the intellectual merits of Taylor's argument, but would argue that living without any fixed reference points or big pictures has the advantage of offering people complete freedom. Some sections of Western culture now believe that personal freedom allows us to override intellectual integrity, holding that we must be at liberty to choose our beliefs and values without being controlled or influenced by any external constraints. Something can be true for us without being true in itself.

Yet there's a real problem with this position. Our views become nothing more than personal constructions if they are not grounded in anything beyond our desires or our loyalties to our in-groups or influencers. As the German poet Hermann Hesse (1877–1962) pointed out, this was the problem that developed during the period of the Weimar Republic, when culture was rooted in little more than the 'intellectual fashions' and the 'transitory values of the day'.[15]

Perhaps more importantly, humans are prone to invent worlds that fit with their own tastes and vested interests. We allow our desires to determine the reality in which we believe instead of allowing what we believe to shape our desires. Although many argue that religion is the classic example of this process of inventing our own illusory worlds – what Sigmund Freud (1856–1939) famously styled 'wish-fulfilment' – the same applies to atheism, which for many people reflects a desire that there should be no God.

The philosopher Thomas Nagel (b. 1937) was quite clear that this desire lay at the heart of his own atheism: 'It isn't just that I don't believe in God, and, naturally, hope that I'm right in my belief. It's that I hope there is no God! I don't want there to be a God; I don't want the universe to be like that.'[16] Nagel's atheism is really a rationalization of his more fundamental desire for a godless universe.

There is a sense in which Christianity can be seen as a 'counter-narrative' that challenges certain ways of thinking once prevalent in classic Jewish, Greek and Roman culture, as well as many that are influential today. During the 1930s, the Swiss theologian Emil Brunner argued that theology had what he called an 'eristic' task.[17] What he meant by this was that theology did not simply set out its own positive ideas and values; it challenged their alternatives such as Nazism and Marxism-Leninism, the two great secular ideologies of that period. Yet Brunner's approach can easily be applied to rival views of God. For example, the Christian doctrine of justification rejects any idea of a God who is indifferent to our suffering and anguish, or who demands that we achieve moral and spiritual excellence before we can be loved and accepted by God.[18]

We'll consider these points further, particularly in the fourth, fifth and sixth chapters of this book. But we need to move on and think about the rich vision of faith that Christianity articulates before using this as a lens through which we can see ourselves and our world in a new light.

2

Theology as a 'big picture'

There's growing awareness of the cultural importance of 'big pictures'. Some world views are political – such as Marxism and the new far-right ideologies that have emerged in the early twenty-first century – and anyone interested in trying to make sense of the world today needs to come to terms with these ways of thinking and their impact on people. As we've seen, Christianity also gives rise to a big picture of reality and, in this chapter, we'll reflect further on its importance.

Back in the early 1970s, I came across a research paper written by the theoretical physicist Eugene Wigner (1902–95), exploring the question of why mathematics seemed to map the natural world so effectively. At the time, I was a science undergraduate at Oxford and I shared Wigner's sense of puzzlement about the ability of pure mathematics to help us in our search for the 'ultimate truth'. Why does mathematics, which is meant to be the free creation of the human mind, track the contours of reality so well?

What really interested me about Wigner's paper, though, was the way in which he defined 'ultimate truth' as 'a picture which is a consistent fusion into a single unit of the little pictures formed on the various aspects of nature'.[1] It made a lot of sense to me that each aspect of nature or individual scientific discipline offers us a 'little picture'. Science aims to bring all these little pictures together into a coherent big picture so we can see how they are interconnected. It's like a panoramic view of a rich landscape, which holds together snapshots of forests, rivers, roads and villages and thus gives us a more coherent view of reality.

Wigner offered a powerful vision of how science works. And as I began to read C. S. Lewis seriously around that time, I found that he developed a very similar approach in thinking about faith. For Lewis, Christianity sets out a big picture of reality, which can both enfold and hold together the scattered and disconnected elements of our world. Christians actually 'enjoy their world picture, aesthetically, once they have accepted it as true',[2] an insight that links theology with spirituality and worship, to which we shall return later.

I was captivated by the way in which Lewis engaged with theology and began to dream of studying the discipline myself as a means of enriching my faith through entering and inhabiting the imaginative and intellectual landscape that Lewis had sketched for his readers. Happily, things worked out for me. And that's why I wrote this book.

Christian doctrines: isolated or interconnected?

At the beginning of my study of Christian theology, I thought of it as a series of separate and isolated compartments, each containing a single doctrine. This idea is encouraged by theology textbooks – including my own! For example, my bestselling *Christian Theology: An Introduction*, based on lectures I originally gave at the University of Oxford in the 1980s and 1990s, has ten self-contained chapters dealing with specific doctrines such as creation, salvation and the Trinity.

Unfortunately, this educational approach, which aims to make it easier to study theology in a manageable way, can too easily be misunderstood as a statement about the nature of theology itself. It suggests that theology is a set of disconnected ideas, a patchwork quilt of beliefs that are essentially unrelated to one another, like snapshots randomly stuck into a photo album. It's not particularly helpful.

Theology is best seen as an interconnected web of ideas, enfolding spirituality, biblical studies, apologetics and ethics. The doctrine of creation, for example, is linked with other leading themes of faith. We can't speak about the identity and significance of Christ without reflecting on the nature of God, salvation or the Christian life, to mention just the more obvious topics, to which others can easily be added. Theology's big picture is able to fit seemingly disparate snapshots within its panoramic vision of reality. Each snapshot is important and is to be treated with respect, yet each discloses only part of a greater whole.

The Christian big picture, which theology tries to put into words, can give shape and expression to ideas and experiences that might otherwise seem unrelated and disconnected, spilled and scattered throughout our world without any apparent meaning or significance. The Christian understanding is sufficiently capacious to be able to frame and hold complex issues such as the problems of uncertainty and suffering.

One of the reasons I find the history of theology so interesting is that it allows us to see these big pictures being developed and checked out by theologians in the early centuries of Christianity. The first Christians believed in a grand vision of reality, which could be expressed as a set of individual disconnected doctrines yet, ultimately, was far more than these.

There's a very interesting parallel here between the development of Christian theology and scientific theories. In science, you assemble all the observations that need to be explained and try to find a theory that seems able to fit them all in. The Greek word *theoria*, from which our word 'theory' is derived, really means 'beholding' or 'seeing'. A theory is like a thread that links together observations so that they can be viewed as interconnected parts of a greater whole. The quest, therefore, is to find the best interpretation of these observations.

The 'big picture': weaving things together

How is this Christian big picture put together? One of the theologians I got to know as I began to study theology was J. I. Packer (1926–2020), who moved to Canada in 1979 to become professor of theology at Regent College, Vancouver. As an evangelical theologian, Packer stressed the fundamental importance of the Bible for Christian theology. Yet he made it clear that it wasn't enough to know individual biblical passages or themes, offering this advice to anyone reading the Bible for the first time: 'Get the big picture. Don't worry too much at first about specific sentences you don't quite understand. The details fit when you've got the big picture.'[3]

This idea of finding the big picture that makes sense of individual details helps us to understand the development of early Christian theology, especially in the Greek-speaking church of the eastern Mediterranean area in the third and fourth centuries. Cyril of Jerusalem (*c.*313–86) set out an important account of the role of theology and the creeds in his series of Catechetical Lectures given around the year 350 to those who were about to be baptized.

Cyril pointed to the complexity of the biblical witness and the need to enfold this within a coherent framework that enabled the 'teaching of the faith in its totality, in which what really matters is gathered together from all the Scriptures.'[4] Thus, theology is about amassing and integrating the various components of this biblical witness. In explaining Cyril's approach to my students at Oxford, I often used the analogy of weaving biblical threads into a theological tapestry. Each thread is valuable, but the overall picture they disclose is more important still.

This line of thought leads us to an important conclusion. Yes, theology is biblical, but it is *more than biblical.* Theology can be understood as discerning the big picture that holds together the complex biblical witness. Yet this grander vision of things is not itself *directly* disclosed in the Bible; it is *created* by bringing together the multiple biblical threads in our minds and discovering the overall pattern that they reveal when woven together. The pattern itself is not observed, but what is observed points to it. We gaze at the threads and weave these together in our minds to create the framework that naturally and legitimately holds them together.

This helps us to understand the importance of coordinating doctrines such as the Trinity. Evangelical rationalists of the late sixteenth century, such as the Italian writer Fausto Paolo Sozzini (1539–1604), argued that the doctrine of the Trinity was not biblical, in that it wasn't formally stated in the Bible. Others, such as John Calvin (1509–64), responded by arguing that the doctrine of the Trinity was biblical, in that it set out the big picture of God, which, though not fully disclosed by any single biblical statement, is implicit when individual statements are held together in a coherent whole.[5]

Understanding theological disagreement

During my period as a scientist researching aspects of biological membranes at the University of Oxford in the mid-1970s, I regularly found myself confronted with a set of experimental results that could be interpreted in different ways. Usually, there are several possible theoretical interpretations and the challenge is to choose which is the best interpretation of your observations. The issue is known as 'inference to the best explanation' in the philosophy of science and a number of solutions have been developed.[6] For example, the simpler and more elegant the theory, the more likely it is to be right.

John Polkinghorne (1930–2021), a professor of mathematical physics at the University of Cambridge, who later turned to the study of theology, saw clear parallels between the intellectual endeavours of theologians and of scientists. While the scientist aims to find the simplest and most elegant theory that would account for the observational evidence, the theologian aims to find the simplest and most elegant theory that would take account of the biblical 'record of persons and events through which the divine will and nature have been most transparently made known.'[7] For Polkinghorne, the classic Christian notions of the Incarnation and the Trinity are the most satisfying framework for holding together the complex biblical witness.[8]

The quest for the larger vision underling the New Testament was particularly important in the first phase of Christian theology, especially in the great theological centres of Alexandria in Egypt and Antioch in Asia Minor. How could intellectual and imaginative justice be done to the ideas and practices deriving from the New Testament and the apostolic era? If we think of these as threads, what possible patterns might result from weaving them together? And how do we decide which is the *best* pattern, the most authentic?

Such questions help us to understand why theologians can disagree on issues. This is a well-known problem in other fields, including the sciences. For example, think of the debate that has been going on about whether the observational evidence points to a single universe or to a group of universes (the 'multiverse'). There is evidence for both these views but it's not conclusive. Scientists know this and have learned how to disagree graciously while they wait for conclusive evidence to resolve the debate.

In theology, the problem is often focused on two particular issues: how individual biblical passages are to be understood and how multiple passages are best woven together into a big picture. A good example of the first disagreement is the sixteenth-century debate between Martin Luther (1493–1546) and Huldrych Zwingli (1484–1531) over how to interpret Christ's words, spoken when holding bread at the Last Supper: 'This is my body' (Matt. 26.26). For Luther, this meant that the bread in a Communion service *was* Christ's body; for Zwingli, it meant that it *signified* Christ's body. For Luther, Christ was thus present (in some sense) at a Communion service; for Zwingli, Christ was remembered in his absence.[9]

When I taught on this debate in my lecture course on the theology of the Reformation back in the 1980s and early 1990s, I would explain how each of these theologians arrived at their interpretation, how they dealt with objections to it and what the consequences were. Although I had my own views on the matter, I felt that it was important to be fair to both Luther and Zwingli and leave it to my student audiences to make up their own minds.

Finding the best 'big picture'

This debate between Luther and Zwingli, however, focused on interpreting a single biblical text. More often, theological debates concern how best to weave together multiple texts from the New Testament. A good example is the fourth-century argument at Alexandria between Arius (256–336) and Athanasius (*c.*296–373) about the identity of Jesus Christ. We'll look at this, as it deserves close attention.

Arius took the view that Christ was a spiritually privileged human being; Athanasius that Christ was God incarnate. For Arius, Christ was 'first among the creatures' – he was like the rest of us, but much better. For Athanasius, Christ was both divine and human, with a unique capacity to mediate between God and humanity and to transform the human situation. Both Arius and Athanasius were able to present their very different theories as defensible ways of interpreting the biblical texts, yet this criterion, *on its own*, proved inadequate to determine who was right.

For Athanasius, there were individual biblical texts that pointed to the humanity of Christ, but there were other texts that required an expansion of this insight about his identity.

For example, the New Testament spoke of Christ as our 'Saviour', yet it was widely agreed within Judaism that God alone was able to save. Athanasius argued that the only way to weave all the New Testament insights together into a coherent whole was to think of Christ as having two natures: human and divine.

In reaching this conclusion, Athanasius also appealed to the tradition of worshipping Christ, already evident in the New Testament and continued in the Church's regular worship. If Christ was not divine, Christians were guilty of idolatry (worshipping someone or something that was not divine). Athanasius won this debate because he was able to show that his account of the identity and significance of Christ was theologically coherent and completely consistent with this core Christian practice inherited from the time of the apostles. The important point to appreciate is that the same set of observations can, and do, legitimately give rise to different theories, leading to debates about which big picture makes the most sense of them.

Another point worth noting here is the way in which Athanasius reads the New Testament. For him, Christian theology involves approaching the text with respect and seriousness, trying to grasp the unity that lies behind the plurality of its statements. Whereas biblical scholars might focus on trying to understand the structure and language, Athanasius wants to uncover and safeguard the New Testament's depiction of Christ, whether this is explicitly stated or subtly implied.

We might think of a distinction expressed by C. S. Lewis in his 'Meditation in a Toolshed': 'You get one experience of a thing when you look along it and another when you look at it.'[10] Biblical scholars look *at* the text; theologians such as Athanasius look *along* the text, trying to grasp the reality that brought it into being in the first place and how this might be put into words. Or, to express this another way, those who look at the biblical text do not necessarily see what the text is talking about or pointing to. Those who look along the text, however, aim to enter into its strange and wonderful new world. Both approaches are important, but they are different.

For Athanasius, the doctrine of the 'two natures' – that Christ had to be understood as both human and divine – was the best framework for making sense of the complex New Testament witness. It respected its multiple aspects on the one hand, and held them together in a coherent whole on the other. The complexity of this biblical witness to Christ had to be respected rather than reduced or simplified. For Athanasius, the coming together of the divine and human natures in Christ is the basis of the salvation of humanity, enabling God to heal a sinful and wounded human nature. Christ is not to be seen simply as some kind of human religious teacher telling us about God, he also *shows* us what God is like and, because he is God incarnate, he is able to *save* us, not merely to instruct us.

This view was endorsed by the Council of Chalcedon in 451, which most Christians see as a landmark in self-understanding. As the German Catholic theologian Karl Rahner (1904–84), remarked, the Council of Chalcedon really denoted the beginning, not the end, of orthodox Christian discussion of the significance of Christ by clarifying the boundaries within which such discussion took place.[11] Chalcedon, however, did not resolve the question of how the 'two natures' were to be visualized. Should we think of them as somehow existing side by side in Christ? Or did they exist in a closer, more integrated manner?

In the end, most early Christian writers seem to have concluded that what really mattered was affirming the reality of the humanity and divinity of Christ and defining the broad limits of what counted as orthodox Christologies. If you like, Chalcedon tried to fence off a broad area of theological territory that was 'orthodox'. In fact, this allowed a 'generous orthodoxy' that both recognized what is definitive and identity-giving and allowed gracious debate and discussion to take place.[12]

But what difference does this make? I'm often asked by people who are looking in on Christianity from the outside to explain why the debate about the identity of Christ actually matters. Let's look at this point, using the novelist Dorothy L. Sayers (1893–1957) as our guide.

Dorothy L. Sayers on the Incarnation

As we've seen, the Christian big picture provides an interpretation of the world and our place as human beings within it, which informs our thinking about how we ought to live, modelled on Christ. But why *Christ*? Why not someone else?

Dorothy L. Sayers explored this question in a lecture in May 1940, when her reputation as one of Britain's two premier lay theologians (alongside C. S. Lewis) was at its height. Although Sayers is now remembered mainly for her detective novels, featuring the aristocratic amateur sleuth Lord Peter Wimsey, she was also a literary scholar who translated Dante's *Divine Comedy* and was highly regarded as a capable interpreter of Christian theology for a wider readership.

Sayers framed her question in a dramatic way: why look to Christ rather than Adolf Hitler as an exemplar of what Christians understand by an authentic life? Her audience might have been shocked by the comparison. After all, Britain was at war with Germany at the time and many would have seen Hitler in very negative terms. But Sayers's point is fair and important: we need to be able to identify someone who is qualified to model a 'good life' for us so that we can learn from him or her. And that is a *theological* question.

Sayers declared that it is 'useless for Christians to talk about the importance of Christian morality, unless they are prepared to take their stand upon the fundamentals of Christian theology.'[13] If we choose to imitate Christ because we happen to like the values that he teaches and embodies, we make Christ's authority dependent on our value judgements. For Sayers, there has to be something about Christ himself that makes him the guide to the virtues Christians should be pursuing:

> It is quite useless to say that it doesn't matter particularly who or what Christ was or by what authority he did those things, and that even if he was only a man, he was a very nice man and we ought to live by his principles: for that is merely Humanism, and if the 'average man' in Germany chooses to think that Hitler is a nicer sort of man with still more attractive principles, the Christian Humanist has no answer to make.[14]

Perhaps because of the wartime context, Sayers made her point more forcefully than was strictly necessary. Yet it is significant: there has to be some quality about Christ that makes *him*, rather than *someone else*, the definitive role model for Christians in the life of faith.

Sayers locates this quality in his unique identity, disclosed in the New Testament and given more formal expression in the Christian doctrine of the Incarnation: 'If Christ was only man, then He is entirely irrelevant to any thought about God; if He is only God, then He is entirely irrelevant to any experience of human life.'[15] Christ's authority as a teacher thus rests in who he is rather than our subjective judgement about his teachings. Sayers wants us to realize that the location of Christ within a Christian big picture justifies our belief that he is able to model for us how we ought to live and what we ought to value as Christians. Christ *shows* us what God is like rather than merely *tells* us about God.

Let's develop this approach further by looking at God through the window provided by the doctrine of the Incarnation. What difference does it make to the way we think about God? I've chosen this example because it is important to me personally. One of the factors that fueled my teenage atheism was my belief that God was a total irrelevance. God was in heaven; I was on earth in the midst of time and space. God was not involved or present in my world and had no connection with my situation.

Then, in my first term as a student at the University of Oxford, I learned about the Christian doctrine of the Incarnation. I could see at once that, if this was right, it was a game-changer. God was not a distant irrelevance, an abstract declaration, but one who chose to enter into my world of space and time in personal form. God came to us in order to bring us to God. Now there is much more that needs to be said about this idea and we will return to it later, but the important point is that it gives us both a new way of *thinking* about God and *visualizing* God. Christians hold that they can see the face, not merely know the character, of our God. God is like Christ, who is the 'image of the invisible God' (Col. 1.15). If we are asked what God is like, we can point to Christ, who is – if I can put it like this – the authorized disclosure of God's nature and face.

Mapping the landscape of faith

I introduced the image of a 'landscape of faith' earlier in the book and noted that many Christian writers have suggested theology aims to map this landscape and then help us to explore its individual features. C. S. Lewis uses such an approach: 'Theology is like a map . . . Doctrines are not God: they are only a kind of map. But that map is based on the experience of hundreds of people who really were in touch with God.'[16]

When I was an atheist, I tended to think of Christian faith as the notional acceptance of the terse and dull statements of the creeds. I didn't understand that the creeds were, in fact, maps inviting us to discover and encounter what they were pointing to. God is the one in whom we trust. Theology helps us to find God by mapping the pathways that lead to God and sketching the landscape of how Christians have experienced, visualized and comprehended this God.

While it is helpful to think of theology as mapping the landscape of faith, this can be misunderstood. For a start, we must not confuse a map with the landscape itself. A piece of paper or a digital image can never fully accommodate the beauty, complexity and vastness of a mountain scene.

Nor can a map capture or elicit the experience of 'rapturous amazement' (in the words of Albert Einstein (1879–1955))[17] that such vistas so often evoke as we behold them. Maps help us to find, enter and explore those landscapes, but they can't adequately capture their depth and detail or the impact that they have on the way we think and feel.

Earlier, I mentioned the philosopher Mary Midgley, whose later works are severely critical of those who try to reduce a complex reality to something that is intellectually manageable, or filter out aspects of that reality they find irritating.[18] Midgley counters this reductionism using the helpful image of 'mapping' reality. We have to face up to the fact that the many levels and aspects of our world can never be completely captured by any single map or theory (such as science).

Midgley's point is really helpful theologically: the quality of our thinking ought to be as deep and complex as the realities we hope to understand. That means we have to *struggle* to make sense of God and our universe if we are to avoid what C. S. Lewis called 'a glib and shallow rationalism'[19] in which everything is conveniently and simplistically forced into a mould determined by unaided (and culturally influenced) human reason.

Although Midgley's criticisms were directed primarily against Richard Dawkins's aggressive scientific reductionism, her concerns have a wider significance. To represent God and our world properly, we need to use multiple maps and work out how to superimpose them so that we benefit from their multiple insights and see how they connect up with one another. For Midgley, since every map is necessarily fragmentary, we end up using a 'collection of maps, all of them incomplete', which together build up a 'composite picture' mirroring the complex reality that we are trying to grasp and represent.[20]

This idea of mapping is especially helpful in thinking about how Christians should understand salvation. The New Testament uses a rich range of images to illuminate the many aspects of the Christian idea of salvation, including some drawn from the cultic world of the Old Testament (sacrifice), the law courts (justification), Roman family law (adoption) and personal relationships (reconciliation).[21] One mapping of salvation locates the significance of Christ's death within the sacrificial system of the Old Testament, emphasizing his continuity with the religious practice of Israel, while at the same time proclaiming the end of its validity for Christians. Another conceptual map is offered by the notion of 'adoption', which stresses the new relational and legal location of believers within the family of God and the community of the Church.

Each of these maps offers its own distinct perspective on the nature of salvation while making no claims to ultimacy or exclusivity. None is complete in itself; it offers a partial account of a great reality. As Midgley puts it, 'No map shows everything. Each map concentrates on answering a particular set of questions. Each map "explains" the whole only in the sense of answering certain given questions about it – not others.'[22] The task of theology is to weave these maps together, respecting the distinct contribution that each makes to our understanding of the greater whole so that the richness of the Christian understanding of salvation can be fully appreciated. We shall explore this point further in Chapter 4.

Theology helps us to maintain the unity of the Christian faith while at the same time identifying and respecting its many aspects and elements. It seeks to preserve each of these aspects of Christian belief and appreciate them individually. I've often used an analogy drawn from the history of science when exploring this point with my students. Think of Isaac Newton's famous experiment of 1665, conducted in his rooms at Trinity College, Cambridge. Newton (1643–1727) passed a beam of sunlight through a prism and discovered that it was converted to a spectrum of colours – red, orange, yellow, green, blue, indigo and violet. White light turned out to be complex, made up of multiple components, each of which could be separated out and studied individually. But these components are all part of a greater and richer whole and, as Newton discovered, they can be recombined to re-create the original beam of white light.

Christianity is a unitary whole, a single big picture, but it is rich and complex and calls out for exploration, appreciation, celebration and application. Theology helps us to zoom in and appreciate the detail (the colours) and zoom out to see how everything holds together (the beam of white light). That's why it's such a rewarding undertaking.

But not everyone would agree with that judgement. In the next chapter, we'll look at five significant criticisms of theology and consider what might be said in response to these.

3

Theology: five criticisms

Theology has its critics. Before we begin to explore the benefits and outcomes of our subject, we must pause and listen to these criticisms. Perhaps because I have a high profile as a Christian theologian, many people write to me explaining their difficulties with theology. Sadly, I rarely have enough time to respond properly, but I always make a note of the problems and try to address them in my writings. In what follows, I will look at five concerns. Most of these have been raised by Christians. The first, however, is widely encountered within Western culture.

Theology is vacuous nonsense, which isn't worth studying

Many in the West can see no reason why any intelligent or informed person would want to study theology. I used to share such an outlook, so I will try to explain why I think that this criticism can be countered. Theology matters for serious atheists. It sets out what Christians believe, why they believe it and how they came to express these ideas in certain specific ways. If you want to criticize Christianity intelligently and responsibly, you need to grasp its fundamental tenets. That makes it possible to have productive and helpful conversations between Christianity and its critics on the one hand, and those who are wondering what it's all about on the other.

Engaging with the leading atheist Richard Dawkins helped me to understand why theology matters. Our first encounter was in a private debate at the University of Oxford, in which he argued that science and science alone is able to answer all life's important questions. In 2003, I researched and wrote a theological analysis and assessment of his views about science and Christianity (published the following year), mapping out some of his criticisms of faith and developing responses to those concerns.[1] Before criticizing him, I wanted to make sure that I had understood him.

In 2006, Dawkins's highly influential book *The God Delusion* was published, now seen as the leading manifesto of the movement known as the New Atheism, which fizzled out ten years later. My wife and I wrote a response to Dawkins's critique of Christianity, expressing concern about the shallowness of his understanding and offering a response to his criticisms of faith.[2]

Here's my point: theology sets out what Christians believe and that's important for any public discussion on matters of faith, whether you think Christianity is right or wrong. If you want to criticize Christianity, fair enough – but make sure that you know what it actually is. Dawkins's refusal to take theology seriously means that his criticisms of Christianity are largely based on misunderstandings, misreadings and (sadly) what often seems to be prejudice. As the cultural and literary critic Terry Eagleton (b. 1943) pointed out in a withering review of *The God Delusion*: 'Imagine someone holding forth on biology whose only knowledge of the subject is the *Book of British Birds,* and you have a rough idea of what it feels like to read Richard Dawkins on theology.'[3]

Most atheists I know consider it important to grasp at least something of this theological vision, whether they agree with it or not. Not Dawkins, however. Dawkins's criticisms of Christianity suggest both that he knows little about it and that he relies upon his intended readership to share his ignorance of theology and cultural distaste for faith. I have been astonished at how many people I've met whose understanding of Christianity has been shaped by Dawkins's caricatures. It's hardly surprising that such people crumble and crumple in discussion with intelligent and informed Christians.

The contrast on this point between Dawkins and the leading American evolutionary biologist Stephen J. Gould (1941–2002) is striking. Gould did not allow his personal agnosticism to interfere with his concern to understand what he did not agree with. He took theology seriously, realizing that it represents an important and significant attempt to make sense of our world and our place within it.[4] For Gould, science develops theories to explain the observed facts of nature; theology deals with questions of human meaning and moral values. We need both these fields of knowledge to cope with life.

Dawkins's critique of theology rests on his 'scientism' – the belief that science alone can answer life's great questions. As many of his critics, religious and secular, have pointed out, his sectarian approach to human knowledge is a hopelessly blunt instrument, which wipes out not merely theology but also other significant areas of intellectual and cultural life, such as philosophy and poetry. The cultural critic Neil Postman (1931–2003) put his finger neatly on the problem that many people have with this inflated estimation of the capacities of the natural sciences:

> Science does not provide the answers most of us require. Its story of our origins and of our end is, to say the least, unsatisfactory. To the question, 'How did it all begin?', science answers, 'Probably by an accident.' To the question, 'How will it all end?', science answers, 'Probably by an accident.' And to many people, the accidental life is not worth living. Moreover, the science-god has no answer to the question, 'Why are we here?'[5]

As I mentioned in the Introduction, Dawkins's view is now widely regarded as intellectually circular and imaginatively deficient. It presupposes its own conclusions. Both philosophy and theology are happily now back in business, offering richer and more satisfying engagements with the big questions of life than Dawkins's unsatisfactory overinterpretations of science.

Theology is irrelevant for most ordinary Christians

Over the years, many ordinary Christians, often with impressive educational achievements, have explained to me how they have been put off theology by what they describe as its 'weird vocabulary', its 'intellectual introversion' and its 'disconnection from the life of faith'. I know what they mean. Theology often uses language that bears little relation to everyday life and seems far removed from that of the New Testament.

Much academic theology appears to be written in a language that excludes ordinary people, engaging with writers few have ever heard of and dealing with questions that hardly anyone considers interesting or important. The Yale philosopher of religion Denys Turner (b. 1942) is one of many to protest against this 'vacuity of thought wrapped up in a theological tribal dialect'.[6] It's not surprising that so many people think theology is pointless.

But let's be fair. Every professional group develops its own distinct vocabulary or jargon. Car mechanics, investment experts and medical practitioners all use terms that seem hopelessly inaccessible to ordinary people, but which they understand perfectly as they go about their professional tasks and compare notes on how to do these better. Most academics use one mode of speaking when facing inwards and another when facing outwards. That's why the media is continually looking for economists, philosophers and physicists who know their professional field yet can explain it to ordinary people in everyday language. This is true of theology as well. Some academic theologians see their role as engaging with the questions and debates of their peers; others – such as myself and Rowan Williams (b. 1950) – see themselves as having a responsibility to engage with wider questions, going beyond the professional guild of theologians.[7]

I fully understand why many Christian laity and clergy are suspicious of academic theology, which so often seems detached from everyday concerns. That's why it is so important to realize that most Christian theologians are passionately committed to the wellbeing of their churches and communities of faith. Throughout its long history, Christian theology mostly has been developed by reflective practition ers – by bishops and pastors anxious to educate their congregations and help them to grow in their faith, and by monastic writers concerned to develop an authentic life of Christian prayer and spirituality for themselves and their colleagues. There is much to be learned from them.

Yet every rigorous academic discipline, including theology, develops what the French call *intellectuels engagés*: public intellectuals, deeply rooted in their own fields, who see it as important to make connections with real-life questions, speaking the language of their audiences and engaging with their wider concerns on the basis of a deep familiarity with their own specialist field.

Many, of course, are irritated by the 'everything can be fixed, trust us, we're experts' posturing of some public intellectuals. But the point is that they represent a vital point of contact between a body of specialist knowledge and practice on the one hand, and the concerns of the everyday world on the other.

In the case of theology, the primary interface between this body of knowledge and practice and a wider community is the weekly sermon or homily preached in churches throughout the world. What is a sermon? At its heart, it's an act of theological translation and application, usually based on reflection on biblical passages that have been read aloud to the congregation. A sermon attempts to lodge some core realities of the Christian faith in the minds and hearts of the congregation, to expand their vision of their faith or to make a connection with a local concern or issue. It's an interpretative performance in which the preacher becomes the link between the wisdom of the Christian tradition and the audience.

Whatever else preachers (whether lay or ordained) may be, they are sources of reflective wisdom and catalysts of personal growth in faith for their congregations. The preacher is someone who, steeped in the riches of the theological tradition, is able to see how this can enrich and inform the local community. I will say more about this when responding to the next criticism that is often levelled at theology.

Theology has no place in the life of the Church

In an increasingly pragmatic church culture, theology is widely seen by denominational managers as a waste of time and effort. Clergy should be taught how to increase church membership, not waste their time studying theology. Churches need leaders who know how to grow their market share and pack more people in. Instead of studying dead writers from the past, we ought to focus on those who are seen to matter in the present – such as media consultants, communications experts and social influencers. Church life is really about being affirming, welcoming and inclusive. Theology has no practical value and just gets in the way of much needed church growth, which alone can save the churches from extinction in a rapidly changing cultural landscape.

This view needs to be questioned. As I come from a medical family, it's natural for me to turn to this important discipline for illumination. Is medicine practical? Of course it is. Yet the *practice* of medicine depends on the knowledge of and ability to apply medical *theory*, such as understanding how the human body functions or how its processes can be affected by certain drugs. The medical practitioner is someone who stands at the interface of theory and practice. Having absorbed a detailed knowledge of the multiple disciplines that are necessary to diagnose and to heal, the practitioner brings this wisdom to bear on each individual patient, learning to explain their diagnoses and offering recommendations in everyday language to win the patient's confidence. And it takes time to acquire such knowledge and expertise. The University of Oxford's medical course, for example, lasts six years.

There are obvious parallels with theology. Christian clergy need a range of skills, one being the ability to apply the wisdom of the Christian faith to the situation of their congregations, above all through preaching. Preachers ought to be deeply rooted in the Bible and the long tradition of interpretation of the biblical text, *and* rooted in their community of faith and able to apply this wisdom to its members. Or to use an image associated with the German philosopher Hans-Georg Gadamer (1900–2002), the preachers' job is to connect 'two horizons':[8] the Christian faith on the one hand, and their congregations on the other. Learning how to do this takes time. It's not a quick fix that can be picked up from a seminar.

Preachers are theologians: people who interpret and apply the Christian vision of life to the situations of those to whom they minister. They may not be academic theologians (though some are). They are, however, unquestionably doing theology in practice: explaining, interpreting and applying the Christian faith. Remember that Karl Barth (1886–1968) developed his theology while he was a preacher in the small Swiss village of Safenwil[9] and that most early Christian theologians have passed down to us collections of their sermons, aiming to connect faith and life. Indeed, several hundred of Augustine of Hippo's estimated 8,000 sermons have survived.

We certainly can learn from reading these works, but perhaps we can learn even more from simply remembering and appreciating that these theologians were *preachers* and saw the interpretation and application of theology as integral to their calling. Today's separation of theology from preaching is as artificial as it is unnecessary. We need to recapture the original sense of theology as embracing preaching, spirituality and pastoral care. That's the way it once was and that, in my view, is the way it ought to be.

Theology seems detached from the Bible

This is a widespread concern for many Christians for whom the Bible is a foundational resource. The Bible is central to Christian life, being read in public worship and in private by many Christians, who often use devotional or scholarly commentaries to gain a deeper understanding of its significance. The public reading of the Bible emphasizes its place in the life of faith. Most traditional forms of worship frame the reading of biblical texts by reciting one of the creeds, which offers a structure of interpretation, and through a sermon, which offers reflection, interpretation and application based on these texts.

It is certainly true that some more philosophical forms of theology interact minimally with the Bible. Perhaps surprisingly, C. S. Lewis rarely engages *explicitly* in any detail with biblical texts[10] although his writings show a deep *implicit* biblical understanding. Early Christian theologians, however, were deeply and explicitly rooted in the Bible, seeing their task as constructing a systematic account of its basic themes and their application to the life of faith. Cyril of Jerusalem, for example, delivered a series of 23 'Catechetical Lectures' around the year 350, each of which explores a text of Scripture before opening up into a wider discussion of Christian beliefs.

Cyril is the norm, not the exception, in his use of the Bible. Many early Christian theological works, whether these took the form of biblical commentaries or works of systematic theology, regularly included extended engagements with biblical texts. This may be one of the reasons for the resurgence of interest in their writers in recent decades, and a growing appreciation of their importance for stimulating theological reflection in the present.

It needs to be appreciated, however, that theology is not the mere *repetition* of biblical passages; these need to be *interpreted* so that they can speak into present debates and concerns. As the leading British New Testament scholar John Barclay (b. 1958) rightly notes:

> Our task in each generation, and in each cultural and historical context, is not simply to preserve these words but to unfold them, to explicate them, to tease out their meaning, in a way that 'masters' – that comes to grips with and persuasively communicates to – our constantly changing present.[11]

Theology weaves together biblical themes and passages so that they can be understood within the larger vision they disclose when taken *together* but do not disclose *individually*. We explored this point earlier when we considered how theology weaves individual biblical themes together to give a big picture of reality.

Barclay also argues that theology 'has no "once and for all" form of discourse',[12] as if it could be stated in a way that is valid for all places and times. It is not enough to repeat the words of the New Testament without explaining what they mean in contemporary language; theological interpretation means translation into the cultural vernacular, which changes over time. Theology aims to communicate what the biblical text means to today's readers in the present.

For Barclay, we have to ask what it would mean to 'speak from and with Paul in ways that resonate in the 21st century', recognizing that some attempts to do this in the past now seem outdated. We need to 'rearticulate Paul's meaning in a way that is genuinely good news for our contemporaries'.[13] That is why we need theology – to enable a constant translation of the realities of biblical faith into language and concepts that connect with today's audiences rather than repeat past articulations of those realities, which may be framed in terms that are now unfamiliar and often open to misunderstanding.

Theology is a Western invention

Today, Christianity is a global religion. Although its geographical heartlands during the Middle Ages were primarily in Europe, it has now spread throughout the world, with many of its more dynamic forms based in Asia, Africa and Latin America. Over the last few decades, my correspondents in southern Africa, the Middle East, India, China and Japan have raised a concern that I think is worth engaging with here. Since theology is a Western invention, it cannot be allowed to have a privileged place in this geographically and culturally expanded Christianity. Why should global Christianity be shaped by a Western ideology?

Indeed, it is possible that certain forms of Christian theology are influenced by their Western contexts and, thus, are unhelpful in African and Asian contexts. Yet theology itself goes back to a period when 'the West' simply did not exist. The importance of this point can be seen by considering the cultural background of two of the most influential Christian theologians, who are regularly cited today as central reference points in theological discussions. In fact, I've already referenced both. It's time to look at them in a little more detail.

The Egyptian theologian Athanasius was born in Alexandria, which was then one of the most ethnically diverse cities in the Graeco-Roman world of late classical antiquity. His writings suggest that he was fluent in both Coptic and Greek. (The ancient Egyptian Coptic language was displaced by Arabic as the primary language of Egypt following the Muslim conquest of the region three centuries later.) Today, Athanasius is one of the most cited and engaged with theologians and his seminal work *On the Incarnation* is seen as a landmark in the development of theology.

Augustine of Hippo was born in the territory of Numidia in North Africa, which was populated by three main people groups: indigenous Berber tribes, the descendants of Phoenician immigrants from the eastern Mediterranean and Roman immigrants. Augustine is generally thought to have been a Berber, who was converted to Christianity during a period spent in Italy before his return to Numidia, where he became bishop of Hippo Regius (now part of the city of Annaba in modern-day Algeria). Long after his death, Augustine played a pivotal role in the great medieval theological renaissance in western Europe, which helped to consolidate Christianity as both a private belief system and as a public world view.

While Christian theology today includes significant contributions from Western writers, its historical roots and most significant classical 'influencers' lie in what is now the Middle East and North Africa. Some, sadly, dismiss theology as the outdated reflections of the dead. This shallow judgement fails to appreciate how much we can learn from those who have, in the past, wrestled with Christianity's core vision in trying to illuminate and transform their situations. Yet, happily, modern theology increasingly engages with the wisdom of early Christian writers such as Cyprian of Carthage (*c.*210–258), a Berber born and active in modern-day Tunisia, and Gregory of Nyssa (*c.*335–*c.*395), born and active in modern-day Turkey.

One of the most significant trends in modern theology is the retrieval of the ideas and methods of these ancient writers, including the ways in which they read and understood the Bible, the spiritual and theological 'disciplines' they developed and their potential to illuminate how Christianity can engage with multicultural contexts, such as those of late classical antiquity.[14] They have bequeathed to us a *usable* legacy, which we can quarry, interpret and apply to our own contexts without being trapped in the past.

*

In the first part of this book, I have explored some aspects of theology – emphasizing its importance in securing the core vision of the Christian faith – and the need to appreciate the individual elements of this vision, as well as its coherence. The New Testament says 'in him all things hold together' (Col. 1.17), which allows us to see both the rich diversity of the Christian gospel on the one hand, and its fundamental unity on the other. The gospel is like a multifaceted jewel with many aspects to explore and appreciate and then put to good use.

The second part of the book focuses on how we *use* theology. I've already pleaded for a recovery of the older vision of theology as enfolding the nurturing of the Christian life, focusing on preaching, character formation and spirituality.[15] Theology does more than preserve the core themes of the gospel; it helps us to apply these to the great questions of human existence. In the next three chapters, we shall consider three themes that can be illuminated and transformed by theological reflection: the quests for wisdom, wellbeing and wonder.

Part 2

WHY THEOLOGY MATTERS: WISDOM, WELLBEING AND WONDER

4

Wisdom: discovering the depths of faith

How does theology engage with the deepest questions of human life? For the second-century theologian Justin Martyr (*c.*100–*c.*165), Christ represented both the fulfilment of the Old Testament law and the classic Greek longing for wisdom. Others followed in Justin's footsteps. Gregory of Nyssa and Augustine of Hippo both explored how the gospel connects up with the wider human search for truth, beauty and goodness. Theology did not merely help us to understand our world and our place within it; it was also able to bridge the gap between the Christian faith and the world of human feelings and longings.

Let's reflect more on the various 'worlds' we occupy, drawing on some ideas developed by the philosopher Karl Popper (1902–94).

Karl Popper: the three worlds

Popper stressed the importance of what he called 'ultimate questions', which are vitally important to human flourishing yet lie beyond the reach of the natural sciences. Human beings, he argued, inhabit three distinct worlds.[1]

1. The world that consists of 'physical bodies', such as stones, stars, plants and animals. This is the physical universe that is studied by the natural sciences.
2. The 'mental or psychological world', by which Popper means the world of our 'feelings of pain and of pleasure, of our thoughts, of our decisions, of our perceptions and our observations'.
3. The world of the 'products of the human mind', such as religious and moral beliefs, scientific theories, understandings of the meaning of life, and mathematical constructions such as Newton's theory of gravitation.

Popper's point is that these three worlds are different yet they're all part of the human encounter with reality and they're all in some way connected.

While some criticism can be made of Popper's approach, most people find it really useful. It's certainly helpful in thinking about the value of theology. One of Popper's most important points is that theories (located in World 3) have the capacity to interact with and alter the other two worlds. In other words, 'conjectures or theories' can serve as 'instruments of change'.[2] They help us see our world in new ways and inspire us to want to change it for the better. Although Popper is primarily concerned with scientific theories, his analysis can easily be extended to political or theological engagement. My point is that theology offers us a framework for connecting these three worlds and a way of understanding how this helps us to flourish and live well.

As we shall discover in this second part of the book, theology offers us a distinct way of seeing and understanding both the objective world around us and the subjective world within us. Faith is about accepting and inhabiting this new understanding of ourselves and our world, which helps us to find meaning, value and fulfilment. Just to be clear, we're not talking about some kind of self-actualization or self-fulfillment but, rather, about seeing ourselves in terms of what God wants us to be and is willing to help us become.

Let's now focus on how theology helps us to reflect on the first of our three classic themes: wisdom.

Growing in wisdom: a New Testament foundation

What is the difference between knowledge and wisdom? As the philosopher Alfred North Whitehead (1861–1947) pointed out, someone who is 'merely well-informed' may turn out to be 'the most useless bore on God's earth'.[3] Yes, you need to know *something* to be wise, but it's clear that someone could 'easily acquire knowledge and remain bare of wisdom'.[4] Whitehead sees wisdom as going far beyond the mere accumulation of facts. Wisdom is a 'mastery of knowledge', which enables a wise person to engage with a complex and uncertain world using deep insight and reflective judgement. Whitehead's philosophical judgement can be supplemented by more psychological accounts of wisdom as an integration of knowledge, experience and deep understanding, coupled with a willingness to live with the uncertainties of life.

The sociobiologist Edward O. Wilson (1929–2021) pointed to a sense of despair at the close of the twentieth century as people found themselves overwhelmed with detail, unable to discern any big picture in life: 'We are drowning in information, while starving for wisdom.'[5] For Wilson, we can't see the wood for the trees. Wisdom is about achieving depth of understanding rather than settling for superficial engagement. We need to appreciate the interconnectedness of things rather than focus on isolated ideas. And perhaps most difficult of all, we must come to terms with ambiguity and uncertainty and learn how to cope with a complex universe that refuses to accommodate itself to our demands for simplification.

It's clear that many are questing for something deeper than the ephemeral opinions and values of our day, which so often turn out to be little more than the intellectual posturing of self-important groups being presented as if they were the permanent truths of the future. But this is nothing new. We find the same concerns about shallowness expressed throughout human history, including in the 'wisdom literature' of the Old Testament and the letters of the New Testament. Indeed, early Christianity was widely understood at the time as a 'philosophy' – a love of wisdom, a trustworthy and reliable mode of thinking and living that people were invited to embrace. Early Christian artwork occasionally depicted Christ as wearing a *pallium* (a philosopher's cloak) for this reason.

As I see it, theology is what I like to call 'a reflective habitation of the Christian faith', which is grounded in and nourished by the Bible and the long Christian tradition of engaging with and interpreting the biblical text. There's no doubt that the New Testament takes the believer's cultivation of wisdom with great seriousness, emphasizing that Christ is the one 'in whom are hidden all the treasures of wisdom and knowledge' (Col. 2.3), and criticizing other approaches, such as the self-serving pretensions to wisdom that Paul notes in his Corinthian correspondence (1 Cor. 1.17–20).

For Paul, Christ is the 'wisdom of God' (1 Cor. 1.24), embodying and manifesting wisdom not as a set of abstract principles but as a lived life, which can be a model and encouragement to others. Christ is not, therefore, simply to be understood as a 'teacher of wisdom' but as someone who *embodies* that wisdom.

We know that many early Christian writers, particularly orators and philosophers who were converted from paganism, felt uneasy about (and were possibly embarrassed by) the simple language of the New Testament. It seemed to lack the rhetorical elegance and conceptual sophistication of classic philosophical literature. It's noticeable that the two New Testament letters that show most interest in the conceptual world of wisdom – the Epistles to the Colossians and Ephesians – were perceived as more sophisticated, perhaps because of the greater complexity of their vocabulary and style.

How does theology come into this? A good place to start is Augustine of Hippo's reflections on Christian wisdom. In his important early work, *Instructing Beginners in the Faith*, probably written in 403, Augustine sets out to deal with many of the questions asked by those who were new to the faith and wanted to understand what they had embraced. It's a remarkable work, notable for the clarity of its exposition and the extent to which Augustine discloses his own anxieties and concerns. For example, he confesses his disappointment that he's unable to communicate the excitement that theological ideas had aroused in his mind to his students.[6]

However, Augustine is more concerned with the apparent tension between the simplicity of the New Testament's vocabulary and the rich response the text may be expected to create in its readers as they interpret and assimilate it. Augustine stresses that the main purpose of Christ's life and death was to show humanity the full extent of the love of God and that, having discovered this, people might 'come to be set on fire by the love of the one by whom they were first loved.'[7]

Augustine's point is that Christians are drawn into a transformed mode of living and thinking, which arises because we are drawn towards a loving God. In drawing closer, we gradually come to discover, and then be shaped by, the nature of this God. The desire for wisdom, like the desire for righteousness and holiness, arises from this powerful yearning to be like God, who is the source of all wisdom, righteousness and holiness. Augustine's concern is thus to help evoke a passion within us to reflect the character of God, not simply to explain these ideas and the benefit we can gain from them.

As my Oxford colleague Carol Harrison (b. 1953), one of Augustine's more insightful recent interpreters, remarks, essentially, he 'replaces the "art of delivery" or effective speaking with the "art of reception" or effective hearing.'[8] The simple words of the New Testament thus become the channel through which a more sophisticated and individually adapted vision of wisdom emerges in individuals, perhaps catalysed by the teacher or preacher but ultimately reflecting the transformative work of the Holy Spirit. The simple words of the New Testament draw us into a divine mystery that cannot be expressed in such simple terms yet enthralls and captivates believers, motivating them to want to become like God. Wisdom is not presented here as a tabulated collection of virtuous habits but, rather, in terms of developing a mindset, an integrated Christian framework of thought and action, grounded in and conforming to the example of Christ.

Augustine is aware that people are drawn to Christianity for a variety of reasons, some laudable and others decidedly less so. Yet, perhaps surprisingly, he suggests that someone's motivation to become a Christian or join a church is of little significance. What really matters is that the church is the place in which our desires are converted, in that they are redirected from a lesser good to the supreme good. The task of the Church is to enable this desire to flourish in new believers even if they do not have such a desire to start with.[9]

As Augustine makes clear, Christianity enables us to see things in a new way, with important results for what we consider to be wise thinking and wise acting. The Christian gospel 'heals the eyes of the heart',[10] leading to an imaginative and affective transformation of the way in which we understand ourselves and our world. Augustine sets out the Christian interpretation of the world and the place of human beings within it and offers his own account of how we can and should live well within that world on the basis of this interpretation.

But what is this wisdom? Augustine suggests that it's a recalibration of our desires in the light of who we now realize we really are, and what we really need:

> Holy Scripture speaks like this: 'People are like grass; their glory is like a flower in the field. The grass withers and the flower fades, but the Word of the Lord endures for ever' (1 Pet. 1.24–5). So if anyone longs for true rest and happiness, they ought not to set their hope on things that are mortal and transitory, but rather fix it on the word of the Lord, so that, by holding firm to that which endures for ever, they may endure for ever with it.[11]

How does theology help us to become wise? Even these brief reflections allow us to begin to give some kind of answer. Theology, by setting out a vision of the world and our place within it, helps us to to make decisions about what really matters. It helps us to identify goals in life and how these might be achieved. We need to find ways of bringing together theology and practice in the form of Christian lives that are lived well.[12]

Yet for many, what really matters is escaping from superficial forms of religious faith, which lack any significant depth and grounding. We'll explore this important theme further in what follows.

The wisdom of the Christian past: an antidote to superficiality

One of the downsides of our increasingly scientific culture is a tendency to disparage pre-scientific times. What did anyone then know about anything? The literary critic and public intellectual Alan Jacobs (b. 1958) is one of many writers to question this dismissal of the past.[13] The past teaches us, not least because it allows us to see beyond what our present moment can offer. Reading the classics means allowing someone from another world to speak to us and offer perspectives that might at first seem strange and distant, yet could hold the key to new insights and peace of mind.

As Jacobs points out, this wider cultural principle needs to be heeded by the Christian churches, which so often prize innovation and pay attention only to familiar voices and what brings instant gratification. Theology involves a dialogue with the past. We're not required to retreat into some kind of nostalgic paradise, but we do need to heed the challenge to consider approaches and outlooks that might be new to us but were well known to earlier generations. Superficiality is the abiding cultural deficit of our age, evident in Christianity as in so many other areas of life. That's why taking past writers seriously is so important. Let me elaborate.

'Just trust God and read the Bible!' As I recall, this was the conclusion of a rather dull sermon that I heard preached by a student preparing for ministry. The preacher referenced no one other than himself and offered some rather trite answers to the big questions of life. He had, he told his audience, once had difficulties with the problem of pain, but he had prayed about it and now it didn't bother him any more. Some older members of the congregation were unimpressed and offloaded their irritation on me afterwards. What about the problem of doubt? How were we to make sense of some difficult biblical passages? Their basic complaint was that the sermon was superficial, failing to recognize the genuine problems people experienced in the life of faith. They were hoping for wisdom and, instead, were offered a series of banalities. 'We need more depth than that!'

There's a problem here – not with Christianity itself, but with the calibre of so many of those who preach and teach it. Looking back on my own journey of faith, I now see that I was fortunate in those I chose as my theological mentors. I discovered C. S. Lewis and initially relished his rigorous intellectual and imaginative account of the Christian faith. Yet Lewis served another function for me: he acted as a gateway to a tradition of wisdom, pointing me backwards to writers he had found helpful – such as Augustine of Hippo, G. K. Chesterton, Dante, George Herbert and Thomas Traherne.

As I explored this rich territory of theological wisdom, I found myself being anchored to the past, not in the sense of being restricted and confined by the limits of that past but, rather, in the sense of being connected with a long history of interpretation and reflection on the great themes of faith, from which I could learn.

This discovery of the importance of the Christian past took me by surprise. As a scientist, I was taught that there was no point in reading research articles that were more than ten years old, as the field would have moved on significantly since then. I had grown up in the 1960s and, like many shaped by that decade's ephemeral cultural mood, I saw the past as an irrelevance. Lewis helped me to realize that other Christians had thought about matters of faith for 2,000 years and there might just be something to be learned from reading them. I would still forge my own personal vision of faith, but my ideas would be enriched and given depth by this tradition of reflection.

Initially, Lewis became my gateway to this tradition, identifying sources that I could explore and engage with. When I began actually studying theology, I encountered new names and writers who excited and challenged me. Yet it was when I was reading one of Lewis's later works, dealing with the intellectual virtue of entering fully into the opinions of others in a process of 'good reading', that I encountered an intellectual framework which helped me to make sense of what Lewis both commended and practised:

> My own eyes are not enough for me, I will see through those of others . . . Literary experience heals the wound, without undermining the privilege, of individuality . . .

> In reading great literature I become a thousand men and yet remain myself. Like the night sky in the Greek poem, I see with a myriad of eyes, but it is still I who see. Here, as in worship, in love, in moral action, and in knowing, I transcend myself; and am never more myself than when I do.[14]

Lewis thus did more than encourage me to read the riches of the Christian past and to reject dismissive gestures of 'chronological snobbery', which declared that the past was irrelevant and unusable. He helped me to see that I, as a reflective individual, could overcome the limits of my specific historical location and cultural perspective by tapping into a rich tradition of reflection, which expanded my vision of faith. Christian theology is a corporate undertaking in which the voices of the past have a welcome and necessary place, challenging ephemeral orthodoxies and offering alternatives that demand constant reconsideration.

Having said this, Lewis is not encouraging an *uncritical* acceptance of theological and spiritual ideas of the past (which might contain error and misunderstanding as much as wisdom). His point is that ideas originating in the past *that have been tried and tested* can be retrieved quite easily, dusted off and given a new lease of life in our own thought, which is enriched as a result. I find it helpful to read recent writers who, like Lewis before them, have found certain older writers useful, and note which authors they perceive to be valuable and how they use them.

A good example of this process is found in Rowan Williams's extended reflections on the ideas of Augustine of Hippo. Williams, a professor of theology at the University of Oxford who went on to become Archbishop of Canterbury, offers thoughtful readings of a number of major theologians, highlighting certain aspects of their thought and making fresh connections with contemporary questions. For example, consider this comment on the importance of Augustine's *Confessions* for the human quest for wisdom:

> Left to ourselves, we can fantasize about gaining wisdom by effort, but in fact we shall only be locking ourselves up still further in our illusions, admiring not the eternal wisdom but our own spiritual skills.[15]

Here, Williams underscores three important theological insights. First, wisdom is not something we achieve but something that gradually arises within us as a result of our transformative encounter with the greater reality of God. It is a work of grace, not a human achievement. Second, natural human notions of 'wisdom' are often self-serving and self-referential. We need to be challenged by a new vision of both what it means to *be* wise and how we can *become* wise. Yet there is a third insight, too easily overlooked. Engaging with past writers can illuminate and enrich our present by allowing us to tap into past wisdom that has proved its value over time.

Wisdom is about being rooted in the past – not *retreating* into this past but being able to draw on its insights and put them to fresh use in the present, especially as we face an uncertain future. In her remarkable account of the importance of 'being rooted' for human identity and flourishing, the French philosopher and religious writer Simone Weil (1909–43) highlighted the need for a sense of connection with the past in facing the future:

> Being rooted (*enracinement*) is perhaps the most important and least recognized need of the human soul. It is one of the most difficult to define. A human being has roots by virtue of a real, active and natural participation in the life of a community which preserves in a living form certain treasures of the past and certain expectations for the future.[16]

Theology helps us to grasp a vision of reality, embodied in the community of faith, which is rooted securely in the past, enabling it to retrieve and present the wisdom of the past to the present. Weil helps us to think of the Christian Church as a school of wisdom, providing both context and content for growth in faith.

Going deeper: mapping the Christian vision of salvation

Wisdom encompasses questioning slick and shallow simplicities and respecting complexity. We need to resist the temptation to limit or reduce reality to the intellectually manageable because the truth is that both our universe and God lie beyond our total comprehension. Theologically, this principled attempt to safeguard the depth of reality from shallow interpretations is best seen in the desire to 'preserve mystery' by insisting that we respect its integrity, affirm its fundamental unity and, at the same time, identify its multiple aspects.

As I noted earlier, the philosopher Mary Midgley, who stresses the importance of doing justice to complex realities, suggested thinking of 'multiple maps' to make sense of a rich and deep world. Midgley also suggests that we need to use 'multiple windows' on our world, each with its own angle on reality. She illustrates this idea using the analogy of a large aquarium with multiple viewing windows to allow observers to see each aspect of its extensive underwater habitat:

> We can eventually make quite a lot of sense of this habitat if we patiently put together the data from different angles. But if we insist that our own window is the only one worth looking through, we shall not get very far.[17]

Each window offers us its own distinct and significant view of this greater reality, which is to be valued in its own right and for its own sake while at the same time being part of a greater coherent whole. We need to work out how to bring these partial viewings of the aquarium together.

The New Testament makes use of a number of 'viewing windows' into the rich and complex Christian understanding of salvation. Theologians tend to refer to these as 'soteriological metaphors', meaning analogies or illustrations that help to capture some particular aspect of the Christian understanding of *sōtēria* (salvation), often using language and images that were accessible to ordinary people.[18]

These images and analogies served two important purposes. First, they enabled those who had responded to the Christian proclamation to understand what had happened to them by giving them maps of the new territory of faith they now inhabited. And, second, they served an important purpose, apologetically or evangelistically, in helping to explain the Christian understanding of salvation to those outside the community of faith using accessible cultural analogies, such as a slave being set free or two people being reconciled so that their relationship can be restored and renewed.

There were many religions and mystery cults in the multicultural world of the New Testament, each offering its own distinct account of the nature of salvation and how this could be achieved. Christians needed to be able to explain what was distinct about their own beliefs. Each of the New Testament's 'soteriological metaphors' is like a snapshot of a panoramic view, capturing some – but only some – of its features with particular clarity. Let's look at four of these briefly to help us appreciate this point. Others can be added easily to provide greater depth but, for our purposes, the important thing is to appreciate the diversity of these images and the richness of understanding that they enable.

1 Salvation brings healing to wounded humanity

The Greek term *sōtēria* (normally translated as 'salvation') bears a rich range of meanings, including 'healing', 'restoration' and 'rescue'. There is an important connection here with the healing ministry of Christ, which was entrusted to the early church. Luke records that Jesus gave authority to the disciples to teach and to heal: he 'sent them out to proclaim the kingdom of God and to heal' (Luke 9:1–2). The human predicament is thus understood as that of being ill or wounded and unable to self-heal. The Christian gospel brings healing at multiple levels: physical, social and relational. This point was emphasized by Augustine of Hippo, who compared the Church to a hospital in which the ill and wounded were restored to wholeness under the care of a competent physician.[19] This aspect of the Christian understanding of salvation naturally leads into a reflection on the link between theology and wellbeing. Christianity offers to heal, renew and transform a broken and wounded humanity. We shall explore this point further in the next chapter.

2 Christ is the proper satisfaction for human sin

The context now shifts from a medical to a legal context. The eleventh-century theologian Anselm of Canterbury (1033–1109) argued that a central purpose of the Incarnation was to allow a righteous God to cancel the debt of sinful humanity through 'satisfaction'. Our predicament here is portrayed in terms of being trapped, as we are unable to make the necessary payment or reparation for human sin. By becoming incarnate, God was able to deliver us. Although Anselm's approach has been criticized at points, his fundamental concern was to emphasize that God acted in both justice and compassion to liberate humanity from sin.[20] Redemption was the outcome of God's righteousness.

3 Christ is a sacrifice for human sin

The context now changes again, this time to the religious cult of the Old Testament. The dominant theme here is that humanity is separated from God by the impurity of sin. If we are to be able to draw close to God, this contamination must be purged through an appropriate sacrifice. Christ is depicted, especially in the letter to the Hebrews, as both the sinless high priest and the perfect sacrificial offering, allowing impurities to be cleansed so that people can draw close to God and thus making the sacrificial system redundant.[21]

4 We are adopted into Christ's family by faith

It's important to know that we belong somewhere. This theme of 'belonging' is brought out particularly well by Paul's soteriological metaphor of 'adoption' (Gal. 4.5; Rom. 8.14, 23; 9.4). This image invites believers to imagine their conversion as a transition from belonging nowhere to belonging somewhere and being welcomed, valued and incorporated within a family. We need to appreciate both the legal aspects of this act of social reallocation and redesignation (such as a new legal name and the remission of debts) and also the emotional impact on the person who is adopted. What does this *feel* like?

Someone who was once an outsider becomes an insider, gaining a status and new identity. That person *feels* accepted, valued and potentially empowered. This is a powerful theological theme, which is deftly explored in an early essay by the Yale theologian Miroslav Volf (b. 1956) reflecting on the adoption of his own son and its impact on the birth mother.[22]

These four metaphors all illuminate part of a greater picture of what Christians understand by salvation. What one observer might regard as a series of disconnected and incompatible ideas is seen by theologians as an integrated vision illuminated from multiple perspectives. Different perspectives may be important to different groups. For example, one particular perspective might engage a Jewish readership wondering whether Christianity is inconsistent with Judaism or brings it to fulfilment.

Why is theology so important in reflecting on salvation? Two points may be made in closing this section. First, Christian theology integrates and weaves together the New

Testament's complex witness by insisting that salvation is a rich, multifaceted and *coherent* reality. Each individual aspect is appreciated and acknowledged. It is, however, seen as part of a greater whole, which can only be grasped adequately using multiple windows of perception or described using multiple maps. And, second, growth in faith is about coming to identify, understand and appreciate each of these elements rather than being satisfied with the partial account of salvation offered by only one window or map. Theology thus gives depth to our understanding of the Christian faith.

Making connections: theology and a wider vision of life

Some people express concern that theology is insular and disengaged from the wider world of human knowledge and culture. In fact, wisdom is about making connections and theology is very much about dialogue. It's true that many early Christian writers of the second and third centuries were suspicious of imperial Roman culture, which often saw Christianity as subversive. Today, forms of North American fundamentalism that fear contamination by the secular world often create countercultural communities. Yet there are other ways of inhabiting and engaging with the world.

Most Christians realize that having a robust theological foundation enables and encourages their active engagement with culture, particularly in the areas of literature, art, poetry, politics and ethics. We find this, for example, in writers such as George Herbert, C. S. Lewis, Marilynne Robinson and Dorothy L. Sayers, all of whom frame and ground their literary vision *theologically*. Marilynne Robinson, for example, understands theology to be the 'level at which the highest inquiry into meaning and ethics and beauty coincides with the largest-scale imagination of the nature of reality itself.'[23] What better context could there be for creative writing?

Yet for many, the most important relationship – and potentially the most problematic – concerns Christianity and the natural sciences. The rise of a scientific culture, some argue, is necessarily antagonistic to theology. Yet this is only one option among many. There are certainly points at which Christianity and science find themselves in conflict, particularly if either or both present themselves as complete accounts of reality that leave no space for the other. In the past decade, my own professional career has tended to home in on this intellectual and cultural relationship, focusing on scientists such as Albert Einstein, Stephen J. Gould and Richard Dawkins, who have very different takes on the relation of science to theology.

I believe that a theological perspective affirms the importance of the natural sciences, allowing us to perceive them as a means of enhancing our appreciation of this complex world, which Christians see as God's creation. This perspective helps to explain both the *success* and the *limits* of science. Science is very good at showing how our universe works, but struggles to engage with questions of meaning and value in life.[24]

Over the years, I've developed three main ways of framing the relationship of science to theology, and regularly explore their potential (and their limits) with scientists and theologians who want to bring together their disciplines in an intellectually robust manner. Each way has an imaginative depth and intellectual reach that cannot be conveyed adequately in this short account. None of them is original;

in every case, I draw on existing ideas, even if at times I develop them in new ways.

The first approach is to regard science and theology as offering different perspectives or windows on a complex world (the analogy used by the philosopher Mary Midgley, mentioned earlier). The two perspectives allow us to see different aspects, but neither on its own can do justice to reality.

The second is to regard science and theology as engaging with questions about reality at different levels. In developing this approach, I often draw on insights in the form of 'critical realism' developed by the social philosopher Roy Bhaskar (1944–2014).[25] For Bhaskar, each intellectual discipline engages with reality in its own way and at its own level, which is determined by the nature of its object of study. As Bhaskar puts it, ontology determines epistemology. The nature of an object determines how we investigate it and how much we can know about it. There is no universal method that applies to everything so we have to find out how we can unify or integrate insights developed from different disciplines using their distinct methods.

The third approach also draws on Midgley, who argued that reality is so complicated that we need to use 'multiple toolboxes' to *investigate* it and 'multiple maps' to *represent* it. No single research tool or map is capable of engaging with or depicting reality in its totality; a range of research methods has to be used and their results coordinated somehow – for example, by superimposing different maps so that a richer vison of reality can be attained.

Why is it so important to find ways of framing and encouraging a dialogue between science and theology? Stephen J. Gould gives a good answer to this question in his capacity as a reflective scientist: it is because we 'recognize the different light that each can shine upon a common quest for deeper understanding of our lives and surroundings in all their complexity and variety.'[26] While more could be said on this, Gould helps us to see how theology can help put together a deeper and wider vision of life. For me, theology demands intellectual and personal engagement across disciplines as a means to achieve wisdom, and offers both a motivation and a means to do this.

Faith: being realistic about what we can know

Wisdom, as we have seen, involves respecting complexity and resisting a simplifying reductionism. Yet it is also about coping with uncertainty in life. While we can prove shallow truths – such as '2 + 2 = 4' – the dream of the Age of Reason to establish a set of universal moral and religious beliefs that could be proved to be true is no longer seen as viable. My Oxford colleague Graham Ward (b. 1955) remarked that the Age of Reason demanded that 'we should aspire to knowledge "altogether clear and bright"', characterized by certainty and transparency.[27] Yet this intolerance of uncertainty is now behind us, as philosophy has finally caught up with the limits of human nature. As the philosopher Bertrand Russell (1872–1970) observed, we have to learn to 'live without certainty' yet 'without being paralysed by hesitation'.[28]

A particularly influential TV series in the 1970s was Jacob Bronowski's *The Ascent of Man*, which was widely praised for its account of human cultural evolution. Bronowski (1908–74), a Polish mathematician who was regarded as one of the finest intellects of his age, insisted that the pursuit of human knowledge involves insight and interpretation, going beyond what can be shown to be right. He opened his presentation on 'Knowledge or Certainty' with these words: 'One aim of the physical sciences has been to give an exact picture of the material world. One achievement of physics in the twentieth century has been to show that that aim is unattainable.'[29] For Bronowski, there is no 'God's-eye view' of reality that allows us to answer all our questions definitively and finally: 'Human knowledge is personal and responsible, an unending adventure at the edge of uncertainty.'[30]

So how do we cope with this situation in the life of faith? How can we live out an 'unending adventure at the edge of uncertainty'? This, it has to be said, is a classic theme in both Christian theology and spirituality. Christians think of faith as a journey through an uncertain and puzzling world, trusting in the presence of a God, who accompanies us as we travel. Christian theologians have always been aware of the challenges arising from Paul's declaration that we 'we live by faith, not by sight' (2 Cor. 5.7). To understand how theology might help us engage with this issue, let's look at an approach developed by the American Presbyterian theologian John Mackay (1889–1983) during the 1940s while he served as President of Princeton Theological Seminary.[31]

Like most preachers, Mackay was aware of how images can play a critical role in helping us to organize and coordinate ideas. Drawing on his experience of dwelling in Madrid in the early twentieth century, he developed the images of the 'balcony' and the 'road' as models for the Christian life. Mackay invites us to imagine a group of people who are standing on a balcony, high above a city street, and can see everything below them. They have a God's-eye view of the world. They know where roads lead and what's around the next corner. Yet the observers are onlookers, not travellers. They are detached and distant from what's happening on the road below them. The 'balconeers' – to use Mackay's term – who can overhear the travellers talking, try to work out what they are interested in or worried about. Yet their interest in these problems is purely theoretical; what's going on down there has no relevance for them.

Those who are travelling on the road below, however, see things in a very different way. They are seeking wisdom to illuminate their situation as they travel and to help them become better people. They don't have access to a God's-eye view of the world, which would clarify what life is all about and what the future might hold. There are limits to their knowledge, arising from their location. They have to live with uncertainty.

Mackay's image makes two important points. First, we have to learn to cope with the ambiguity and uncertainty of being on the road rather than being granted privileged access to a God's-eye view of the world. We can't be absolutely sure which of our beliefs really matter, but that's one of the reasons why faith plays a central role in Christian theology!

And, second, Mackay stresses that the community of faith exists on the road, learning and growing as it travels. We learn from one another and from the acquired wisdom of those who have gone before us. The Christian Church is a school of faith, imitating ancient Israel's journey through the wilderness to the promised land, confronted with challenges yet sustained by hope.

We don't learn from those who stand on a balcony, dispensing what passes for wisdom from on high without ever experiencing what life on the road is like. Rather, we learn from the pilgrim community of faith as we travel – the practical wisdom of Christian living that arises from experience and reflection. How do we cope with suffering? How do we relate to others who we find difficult? And how can we grow in our faith in an often puzzling world?

Mackay's contribution to our growth in wisdom is that he offers a way of understanding how we can grow as we journey. And, as I know from many conversations over the years, people do find his framework of the balcony and road helpful. But others want more than this. They're seeking specific guidance on coping with journeying through what so often seems like a dark and hostile world. Let's turn to consider how a significant theologian engaged with this question and what we can learn from that.

The darkness of faith: coping with uncertainty

Throughout this book, I've explored the idea of theology as disclosing an illuminating, energizing and transformative big picture. But what happens if our experience of the world seems chaotic, dark and resistant to interpretation?

Many have a sense today of simply being overwhelmed with information and unable to discern meaning and wisdom. In a sonnet from 1939, the American poet Edna St. Vincent Millay (1892–1950) reflected on the dark events taking place in Europe and the absence of transcendent narratives that might provide anxious American observers with insight and guidance at this time of crisis. It seemed impossible to make sense of things:

> Upon this gifted age, in its dark hour,
> Rains from the sky a meteoric shower
> Of facts . . . they lie unquestioned,
> uncombined.
> Wisdom enough to leech us of our ill
> Is daily spun; but there exists no loom
> To weave it into fabric.[32]

Millay's concern was that she knew of no 'loom' that would allow her weave these 'facts' together so that a pattern of meaning could be seen. No pattern could be discerned or created. How could she live meaningfully in a world that seemed to be meaningless?

This question is important theologically and is often taken up by spiritual writers. For example, we might think of John of the Cross (1542–91) and the 'Dark Night of the Soul'. Another interesting exploration of the theme is found in the early writings of Martin Luther, who achieved fame, both as a theologian and a church leader, during the period of the European Reformation. He was the first major theologian I engaged with in detail as I tried to grasp the core themes of his thought and reflect on their wider significance, so he's important to me personally.[33]

One of Luther's primary concerns was to establish a secure basis for the life of faith in the midst of a troubling and often violent world. For him, the only reliable foundation was the God who was made known in and through Jesus Christ. Luther expressed the point like this in his *Greater*

Catechism of 1529: 'Anything on which your heart relies and depends, I say, is really your God.'[34] Here, we find identified a core belief and attitude, a relationship that defines how we see ourselves and our world. Where others may place wealth, status or possessions at the heart of their lives, Luther argues that personal identity and security are both grounded in and shaped by God, as revealed in Christ.

Yet Luther concedes that God often seems to be shrouded in darkness and mystery in the life of faith. On occasion, like Moses, we seem only to catch a glimpse of God passing in the shadows (Exod. 33.18–23). Luther reminds us that many aspects of the landscape of faith remain shrouded in darkness. How, then, might theology enable us to view this shadowy world?

Luther's answer to this question is found in a series of terse declarations dating from an early period in his ministry at the University of Wittenberg, most notably 'the cross alone is our theology' and 'the cross puts everything to the test'.[35] What did he mean by this? For Luther, the cross of Christ is both the foundation and criterion of faith. While he shares the Christian consensus that the cross is the basis of human salvation, his particular concern here is its subjective impact on believers.

As the behaviour of the disciples makes clear, God was not *experienced* as being present at Calvary, yet subsequent events showed that God was present and active in a hidden way. As Luther points out, we failed to perceive this divine presence and action for several reasons, mainly because of our preconceptions about *how* and *where* God could act. We were looking in the wrong place. Who would have expected God to be present and active at Calvary, a horrifying place of enforced suffering and death, designed to deter anyone from resisting Roman authority?

This is the theological lens that stands at the centre of Luther's 'theology of the cross'. God is present to the trusting believer in darkness and despair, in loneliness and lowliness. In his early lectures on the psalter, Luther was particularly drawn to Psalm 18.11, which speaks of God dwelling in darkness, implying that God is hidden and lies beyond understanding. Luther continued to develop this theme, understanding faith as trusting in Christ even in the midst of a dark world. God dwells in darkness, but is really present to us and for us, despite our inability to penetrate that darkness. We can thus inhabit this darkness, trusting and knowing that God is present in its midst – whether at Sinai, or Calvary, or the ambiguities and enigmas of the life of faith.

Luther, it has to be said, is not entirely consistent in his presentation of the relation between faith and darkness, so we must be cautious about overinterpreting some of his statements. Yet even this brief account of his early theology indicates how it engages with the question of ambiguity and doubt and allows them to be seen in a different manner. Our experience of the absence of God in life may, Luther suggests, represent a misreading of the situation, as in the example of Calvary above, where God was present in a hidden manner. Faith enables us to enter darkness and hold on to the God who is present within. For Luther, this ability to cope with ambiguity and uncertainty is what wisdom is all about.

5

Wellbeing: discerning value and meaning

In August 2005, a few months after his election to the papacy, Pope Benedict XVI (b. 1927) spoke to a World Youth Day celebration in Cologne. He highlighted what he considered to be three of the great questions of the day: 'On whom can I rely? To whom shall I entrust myself? Where is the One who can offer me the response capable of satisfying my heart's deepest desires?'[1] These were matters that everyone could relate to, whether religious or secular.

For Benedict, it was important to convey that Christianity engages with and answers such deep human questions, and that it answers them by pointing to *someone* who can be trusted and is able to satisfy both the desires of the human heart and the questions of the human mind. 'The happiness you are seeking, the happiness you have a right to enjoy has a name and a face: it is Jesus of Nazareth.' For Benedict, Christianity is not merely a map that points us to where salvation and fulfilment may be found; it is about being pointed to the one who makes this fulfilled life possible and shows us what it is like.

Benedict's approach stands in a long tradition of seeing Christianity as both framing and answering 'ultimate concerns' (a phrase popularized by the American theologian Paul Tillich). Christian faith can be understood relationally and existentially. Christ is someone who can be trusted, who will help me face life and live meaningfully. Christ came to bring life – life of new quality and significance: 'I have come that they may have life, and have it to the full' (John 10.10).

Yet, in a provocative but carefully argued recent discussion, the Yale theologians Miroslav Volf and Matthew Croasmun argued that theology seemed to have 'forgotten its purpose: to critically discern, articulate, and commend visions of the true life in light of the person, life, and teachings of Jesus Christ.'[2] A similar point was made by the Princeton theologian Ellen Charry (b. 1947). Charry has shown how many Christian doctrines actually have pastoral goals, in that they seek to shape believers' thinking in 'socially salutary ways'. For Charry, 'to discount the importance of human flourishing is to misunderstand theology and its purpose.'[3]

Some academic theologians would resist any such suggestion, seeing this as the pointless reduction of academic analysis to therapeutic intervention. I don't agree. Anyone who has studied the links between Christianity and healthcare will know that human wellbeing lies at the heart of the ministry of Christ and at the heart of early Christian intellectual and pastoral reflection.[4] From the beginning, Christian theology has set out its own distinct vision of human flourishing, shown how this is grounded in Christ and implemented it in the life of the Church.

For many people in Western culture today, 'wellbeing' is understood mainly in terms of promoting good health and social conditions. Unsurprisingly, many Christian activists are involved in movements working for the elimination of disease and poverty, which, rightly, are seen as major threats to human wellbeing. More recently, increased emphasis has been placed on the importance of mental health, leading to expansions of traditional understandings of wellbeing to include having good mental health, high levels of satisfaction with life, a sense of meaning or purpose and an ability to manage stress. In this chapter, we shall reflect on how theology engages with these important questions.

Theology and wellbeing: the neglected importance of meaning

What is the connection between theology and wellbeing? It's a significant question, given that human beings want more than simply to be able to exist from day to day (though that's an important starting point). They want to know what things mean, to see how they fit together or to discern a big picture that makes sense of the seemingly random events of life. Yet without some informing story, some controlling world view, it proves difficult, if not impossible, to avoid surviving for surviving's sake. Without a transcendent framework, there is no bigger picture, no greater goal.

Theology helps us to decide what is good and meaningful from a Christian point of view. It offers us a framework for leading a 'good' life. However, there is no cultural or philosophical agreement about what it means to be 'good' or to live an 'authentic' life, in that these ideas are shaped by a world view: an understanding of the nature and goals of human beings.[5] As Charles Taylor points out, without an informing big picture, this amounts to little more than 'doing your own thing'.[6]

Back in the eighteenth century, many writers sympathetic to the Age of Reason thought that a universal rationality and understanding of goodness could be achieved. Today, this idea is no longer taken seriously due to the realization that concepts of rationality and goodness are shaped by historical factors.[7] The philosopher Ludwig Wittgenstein (1889–1951) is one of many to point out that what people 'consider reasonable or unreasonable alters'. What people find rational at one point in history is seen as irrational at another.[8]

Yet some would suggest that engaging with the question of meaning in life is really a philosophical question. After all, classical Greek philosophy was clearly concerned with the big questions of life. Why should anyone look to theology to answer such questions? It's a fair point. To answer it, we'll look at the light shed by two significant American voices.

In an autobiographical reflection, the Yale theologian Kathryn Tanner (b. 1957) explains why, as an undergraduate at that university, she shifted her focus from philosophy to theology:

> Theology held for me the prospect of addressing questions of meaning in a comprehensive fashion eschewed by most philosophers at the time. Theology as an academic discipline was clearly about something (not just talk about talk about talk), and its pursuit of the true and the right had significance for a community of inquiry outside itself – the church. Theology, in short, seemed to matter – to someone.[9]

Tanner observes that the 'question of the legitimacy of theology' now seems to have shifted from theology's academic credentials to the question of 'whether theology has anything important to say about the world and our place in it'. We'll come back to Tanner shortly as we look at her helpful views on the identity and significance of Christ.

However, her perception that recent philosophy has not taken seriously the question of meaning is borne out by our second voice, the philosopher Susan Wolf (b. 1952). Wolf observed that this question is rarely raised in professional philosophical circles nowadays, tending to be of interest to young students, whose lack of sophistication causes professional philosophers to cringe with embarrassment.[10] As Wolf notes, talk about life having any meaning now seems to have been 'banished from philosophy'. Happily, however, it is welcomed and remains firmly rooted in Christian theology.

One element of the Christian view of life is that it can be seen as coherent and meaningful – an insight that is highly significant for human wellbeing. The Oxford philosopher Iris Murdoch (1919–99) points out the 'calming' and 'healing' effect of ways of looking at the world that allow it to be viewed as ultimately rational and meaningful. Yet observation, experience and events need to be interpreted if they are to help us understand what, if anything, they mean.

The novelist Jeanette Winterson (b. 1959) highlighted the importance of finding meaning for human wellbeing and dignity in her autobiographical memoir, *Why Be Happy When You Could Be Normal?* (2011):

> A meaningless life for a human being has none of the dignity of animal unselfconsciousness; we cannot simply eat, sleep, hunt and reproduce – we are meaning-seeking creatures. The Western world has done away with religion but not with our religious impulses; we seem to need some higher purpose, some point to our lives – money and leisure, social progress, are just not enough.[11]

Winterson's point is well taken and resonates strongly with much recent research on the importance of big pictures in relation to human wellbeing, and especially the well-established link between meaning and God.

A number of years ago, I was reading the early notebooks of the philosopher Ludwig Wittgenstein, which mainly dealt with some rather dull questions of logic. Yet Wittgenstein's entries for June 1916 show a sudden interest in the meaning of life, a question he saw as linked with the question of God: 'What do I know about God and the purpose of life?'[12] His reflections on this point are rather inconclusive. However, they are important for our purposes as they point to the clear link he intuitively forged between God and finding meaning in life.

So why is finding meaning and purpose in life so important for human wellbeing? This is not a specifically religious or theological question, even though Christian theology answers it in its own distinct way. It is helpful to turn at this point to Michael Steger, the director of the Center for Meaning and Purpose and professor of psychology at Colorado State University. Steger is one of many researchers who has noted that human beings cope more successfully with life's challenges if they feel that they are doing something worthwhile and meaningful.

For Steger, 'meaning' concerns the way in which 'people comprehend, make sense of, or see significance in their lives', along with the manner in which 'they perceive themselves to have a purpose, mission, or overarching aim in life.'[13] Steger points to Viktor Frankl's experience in concentration camps during the Second World War to illustrate how people find ways of coping with suffering and hardship in even the most adverse of circumstances.[14]

Theology contributes significantly to our wellbeing by allowing us to see our world and ourselves in ways that generate meaning and purpose. This is an excellent example of Karl Popper's three worlds being held together within a theological big picture. To speak of meaning in life is to refuse to be restricted to what C. S. Lewis termed a 'glib and shallow rationalism', which limits reality to the realm of empirical facts. It is to reach behind and beyond our experience of this world, to grasp and explore an intellectual framework that positions human beings within a greater scheme of things, and to allow us to see ourselves and our inhabitation of this world in a new way.

Connectedness: discovering a coherent and meaningful world

A core article of faith for me as a teenage atheist was that I inhabited an incoherent meaningless universe devoid of any purpose or significance. *It* was just there; *I* was just there. I had stumbled into a pointless, though often beautiful, world. I loved science, which seemed able to explain how our universe functioned, though not why it existed or, indeed, why there was anything rather than nothing. I was influenced in this respect by the novelist Joseph Conrad (1857–1924), who suggested that the starry brilliance of the night sky spoke 'of the awful loneliness, of the hopeless obscure insignificance of our globe lost in the splendid revelation of a glittering, soulless universe.'[15] The words were elegant yet the message was sombre: there was no point to anything. The universe was a riddle without an answer, an enigma without a solution.

That's not how I see things now. Theology plays a major role in helping us to discern meaning and value in life and, as we've been exploring, one of the ways it does this is by creating a way of looking at the world that is able to bring together what might otherwise seem to be chaotic and disconnected.

This Christian big picture discloses a glorious, loving and righteous God, who creates a world that goes wrong and then acts graciously and wondrously in order to renew and redirect it before finally bringing it to its fulfilment. And we ourselves are an integral part of this story, which discloses our true purpose, meaning and value – who we are, what has gone wrong, what God proposes to do about it and how we are involved in this process of transformation.

The Harvard psychologist William James (1842–1910) made the point that religious faith is basically 'faith in the existence of an unseen order of some kind in which the riddles of the natural order may be found and explained.'[16] Christian theologians have long recognized the importance of making sense of the world and finding its deeper patterns, holding that, in some way, these reflect the wisdom of God as its creator.

However, such reflections lead on to another question. What benefits result from knowing that there is such a 'pattern' or big picture? Let's now reflect on how Christian theology understands the idea of faith and the difference that this makes to us.

Faith: inhabiting a Christian vision of reality

The New Testament's account of the nature of faith is complex, bringing together a range of insights and inviting us to weave them together into a coherent whole. It is theologically tempting to offer a neat definition of faith, but that would necessarily limit our comprehension of it. The Genevan theologian John Calvin suggests that faith is best understood as 'a steady and certain knowledge of the divine benevolence towards us, which is founded upon the truth of the gracious promise of God in Christ, and is both revealed to our minds and sealed in our hearts by the Holy Spirit.'[17]

Calvin's definition is theologically rich, setting his understanding within a Trinitarian context and making a critically important distinction between the objective and subjective aspects of faith. The gospel is both 'revealed to our minds' and 'sealed in our hearts'. Faith is our response to a God who *makes promises* to us – promises that can be trusted and relied upon.

Thus, faith is about entrustment. William Temple (1881–1944), one of Britain's leading theological writers of the early twentieth century, made this point clearly: 'Faith is not only the assent of our minds to doctrinal propositions: it is the commitment of our whole selves into the hands of a faithful Creator and merciful Redeemer.'[18] We see this important theme acted out in Mark's account of the calling of the first disciples, Simon and Andrew, by the shores of Lake Galilee. Mark focuses on the theme of *calling* and *following*: Christ calls; the disciples respond by following (Mark 1.16–18). Christ didn't offer them proof of his identity or importance, or any sort of argument about *why* they ought to follow him. They clearly do not fully understand who this person is or what he wanted them to do or to become. That emerges as they journey with him. As they hear Jesus teach and see him heal and restore, they gradually realize how they fit into his ministry.

To return to our big picture idea, we could say faith is about recognizing that a grander vision of reality exists, that it may be trusted and, finally, it may be inhabited. Like the disciples, we need to step into the world it discloses and make it our own.

This leads us to ask how theology can help us to engage with questions of meaning and the way that we feel about ourselves and our world. To explore this, we'll focus on the central theological notion of Incarnation.

The importance of the Incarnation

In the past few centuries, probably reflecting the influence of the bygone Age of Reason, theology was thought of primarily as making sense of things. Yet early Christian writers saw theology as both enabling understanding and fostering human wellbeing. This can be seen from the works of Augustine of Hippo, who offered a theologically informed account of human flourishing and the pursuit of 'the good life'. In 388, Augustine wrote a treatise comparing the ideas of Christianity with those of the Manichaean sect, to which he had once belonged. One sentence in Augustine's treatise has always stood out for me:

> For if God is humanity's chief good (Latin: *summum bonum*), which cannot be denied, it clearly follows that, since to seek the chief good is to live well, that to live well is nothing other than to love God with all our heart, with all our soul, with all our mind.[19]

Augustine was well aware of the importance of happiness and saw this as inseparably connected with finding and embracing God as both its source and its ultimate goal.

Christianity is an extended imaginative and rational reflection on the significance of its central figure, Jesus Christ, who both *tells* us and *shows* us what God is like: 'The Word became flesh and made his dwelling among us' (John 1.14). The doctrine of the Incarnation speaks of a direct transformative personal encounter between God and humanity that is made possible by the Son of God coming among us, as one of us, in a visible and tangible manner:

> That which was from the beginning, which we have heard, which we have seen with our eyes, which we have looked at and our hands have touched – this we proclaim concerning the Word of life. The life appeared; we have seen it and testify to it, and we proclaim to you the eternal life, which was with the Father and has appeared to us.
> (1 John 1.1–2)

As God incarnate, Christ embodies a life of meaning and value, which Christians are called on to imitate to the extent that they can. Christ *shows* us what the redeemed life looks like as it's lived out in the real world. As the philosopher Ian Kidd remarks, a 'tradition of wisdom' is about more than the 'theoretical articulation of a good life', in that it points to someone who definitively manifests or embodies its 'concrete practical exemplification'.[20]

The Christian understanding of Incarnation also illuminates the search for coherence in our world. The New Testament speaks of Christ as a principle of coherence: Christ 'is before all things, and in him all things hold together' (Col. 1.17). Our fear of meaninglessness is often linked to the perception that there is no 'big picture' in life but, for Christianity, meaning is embodied in Christ as God incarnate. Let's now reflect on the significance of the Incarnation in more detail.

Transforming our existence: mapping the Incarnation

Earlier, in exploring how we might map the Christian understanding of salvation, we discussed the importance of grasping how theology can hold together a rich yet diverse vision of salvation, which has important implications for our wellbeing. Let's now do the same thing for the doctrine of the Incarnation, focusing on the ways in which this doctrine changes the way that we *think* – and *feel* – about ourselves and our place in the universe.

We know that we need to do more than look *at* doctrines; we need to look *through* them, asking how they help us to see ourselves, God and the world. What difference does the doctrine of the Incarnation make to the way that we understand and feel about ourselves as occupants of a complicated world? Let's consider two of the ways in which theologians have articulated these themes.

1 Coping with suffering

Some philosophies see the fulfilled life either as successfully avoiding suffering or denying its real existence or significance. Christianity views suffering as a reality with which we need to engage, and Christian devotional practice often takes the form of contemplation of images of the crucified

Christ. Such images offer reassurance to those undergoing suffering, that their Saviour and God was no stranger to affliction and can be a source of consolation in a time of need. Early Christian spirituality, particularly during the extended period when Christianity was marginalized and sporadically persecuted within the Roman empire, stressed the way in which individual believers' personal stories connected up with the story of Christ, especially in relation to hardship. The wall paintings of Roman catacombs expressed this visually – for example, by depicting Christ as the good shepherd who carried his weary and fearful sheep through a dangerous world.

Many books have been written on how we can make sense of suffering in the world, often treating this primarily as an intellectual riddle that needs to be solved. The rise of rationalism at the time of the Age of Reason (mentioned earlier in this chapter), has led many modern writers to focus on explaining why suffering happens – an undertaking generally known as 'theodicy'. Yet most Christian theologians take the existence of suffering as a given and believe that the question to ask is how faith in a suffering Christ might enable us to *cope* with pain and learn from it.

The American theologian Dorothee Sölle (1929–2003) was sceptical about theological explanations of suffering. In her influential book *Suffering* (1975), she argued that these rationalizations of pain often seemed to do little more than justify the status quo and dull us to the situation of those in anguish. Yet, despite this concern, Sölle believed that it is essential to discern or to create some kind of meaning within what seems to be meaningless suffering if we are to learn from and live well with it. For many Christian theologians, the suffering Christ embodies a real hope that such meaning can be found.

2 Incarnation and attachment

A central theme of classical Christian thinking about the nature of the life of faith is the notion of 'taking hold of Christ' or 'being united with Christ' – two New Testament themes that have found wide theological and spiritual application. Many spiritual writers of the Middle Ages recognized the importance of the theme of 'attachment to Christ', sometimes depicting this as the union of two lovers. In the late twentieth century, however, the theme came to be expressed particularly in terms of 'attachment theory', with its stress on the significance of a 'secure base' (resulting from parental attachment) for the development of a young child. The work of the social psychologist John Bowlby (1907–90) was key here, particularly his 1988 book *A Secure Base*, which highlights the importance of attachment to positive personal development.

This helps us to explore the emotional and relational aspects of the parental care of God embodied in Christ.[21] The American theologian Kathryn Tanner, who, we noted earlier, makes particularly effective use of this image of 'attachment' in *Christ the Key* (2009):

> The Spirit does not merely join us to Christ but, once we are so joined, enters within us as the power for new life according to the shape of Christ's own life as the Son incarnate. We are not just joined to Christ but are to be made over into him by the power of the Spirit we have from him.[22]

Mattering: Christianity and human value

All of us hope that we really matter, that we are, in some sense, special to someone. Yet this hope seems to be subverted continually. Sigmund Freud, for one, famously argued that scientific advance has led to a radical re-evaluation of the place and significance of humanity in the universe, deflating our pretensions to grandeur and uniqueness. We seem so small against this vast cosmic backdrop, which appears indifferent to our presence and wellbeing, that it's easy to be overwhelmed by a sense of our own insignificance.

How might we develop a theological response to this concern? Marilynne Robinson weaves together two theological themes to set these anxieties in a fresh context and allow them to be seen in a new way. One of her most interesting discussions is found in an essay entitled 'Psalm Eight', where she explores existential concerns using some of the opening verses of that psalm:

> When I consider your heavens,
> the work of your fingers,
> the moon and the stars,
> which you have set in place,
> what is mankind that you are mindful of
>   them,
> human beings that you care for them?
> (Ps. 8.3–4)

Robinson's answer to this question has two interconnected elements: we matter because God has created us and we matter because God enters the created order to visit and redeem us.

In the first place, Robinson insists that being created and loved by God confers a status on humanity that, once it is recognized and internalized, reassures us that we are, at least in some sense, *special*:

> The strategy of the Psalmist is to close the infinite distance between God and humankind by confounding all notions of scale. If the great heavens are the work of God's fingers, what is small and mortal man? The poem answers its own question this way: Man is crowned with honor and glory. He is in a singular sense what God has made him, because of the dignity God has conferred upon him, splendor of a higher order, like that of angels.[23]

Robinson then supplements this with a second insight – that this 'infinite distance between God and humankind' is bridged by God in the act of Incarnation in which God 'visits' humanity, entering within our domain and thus gracing it – and us – with glory. That God should consider us worthy of such an act of humility and compassion ought to cause us to reflect on our sense of worth.

A somewhat different approach was taken by the poet-theologian George Herbert in the seventeenth century. We have considered part of Herbert's remarkable poem 'The Elixir' already. In that same piece, he explores the idea of the transvaluation of human life through being 'touched' by God. Here, Herbert picks up on the Gospel narratives of Christ healing individuals by touch, thus restoring them. Herbert likens the graceful 'touch' of God to the famous philosopher's stone of medieval alchemy, which transmutes base metals such as lead into gold:[24]

This is the famous stone
That turneth all to gold:
For that which God doth touch and own
Cannot for less be told.

For Herbert, Christ is the incarnate Saviour who 'touches and owns' believers, thus transforming them. What some consider to be commonplace therefore become precious and significant: they are transvalued by God's grace. This is how *God* sees us, even if we see ourselves more negatively. It's a theme expressed well by Marilynne Robinson in *Jack* (2021), the fourth of her Gilead novels, which calls into question whether anyone can *really* be said to be ordinary: 'You look at a stranger and you see a soul, a glorious presence out of place in the world.'[25] Herbert's 'The Elixir' calls into question cultural assumptions about what is good and valuable and suggests alternatives grounded in a Christian framework.

This theme is developed further by the American Orthodox theologian and novelist David Bentley Hart (b. 1965), noted for his dense writing style and widely admired for the brilliance of his ideas and analyses. Hart argues that 'the Christian vision of reality' amounts to nothing less than a 'transvaluation of all values', in that this vision leads to 'a complete revision of the moral and conceptual categories by which human beings were to understand themselves and one another and their place within the world.'[26]

When Christianity first appeared, some might have seen it as a revolutionary political movement that aimed to overthrow the social structures of its day. Yet, as Hart points out, this was a revolution of the *mind*. It opened up new ways of thinking about God and human beings, which led to many traditional Roman social norms being challenged:

> It is practically impossible for us today to appreciate the magnitude of the scandal that many pagans naturally felt at the bizarre prodigality with which the early Christians were willing to grant full humanity to persons of every class and condition.[27]

Early Christians recognized that their patterns of evaluation and action were to be conformed to the new reality of the kingdom of God and that *everyone* was to be treated well. Why? Because they saw people in a new way, through a new lens. They inhabited a new 'vision of reality':

> The new world being brought into being in the gospels is a world in which the grand cosmic architecture of prerogative and power has been superseded by a new and positively 'anarchic' order: one in which the glory of God can reveal itself in a crucified slave, and in which, therefore, we are forced to see the face of God in the forsaken of the world. In this shocking and ludicrously disordered order, everything is cast in a radically transforming light, and comes to mean something entirely new and perhaps unsettling.[28]

In their very different ways, Herbert and Hart invite us to envisage and put into practice the Christian 'vision of reality', living out a life that reflects the new values it creates and affirms – values embodied in Christ.

What, then, is the point of theology in the light of these reflections? The answer is, it helps us to understand the strange new world that faith both allows us to see and trains us to inhabit, so we can be responsible citizens of this new creation (Phil. 3.20). It enables us to perceive a new moral order, and invites us to align ourselves with its values and live them out in the world in anticipation of the fulfilment of these values in the New Jerusalem. After Christ, we see – and value – things in a new way. As the Italian Franciscan spiritual writer Angela of Foligno (1248–1309) remarked, 'as we see, so we love. The more perfectly and purely we see, the more perfectly and purely we love.'[29]

The Church is the community that sustains this vision of reality and coaches people in the art of living it out. The American theologian Stanley Hauerwas (b. 1940) makes this point well, focusing on the ethical aspects of Christian life.

> The primary task of Christian ethics involves an attempt to help us see. For we can only act within the world we can see, and we can only see the world rightly by being trained to see. We do not come to see just by looking, but by disciplined skills developed through initiation into a narrative.[30]

Hauerwas's point is that a distinctively Christian approach to ethics results from stepping inside the Christian story and reflecting seriously and extensively on how this affects our behaviour. He emphasizes the importance of practicing 'disciplined skills' in order to perceive the world in this new way. What difference does it make to see the natural world and human beings through a Christian theological lens rather than from an atheist standpoint? And who is going to help us to develop these skills and initiate us into this new habit of viewing things?

Inevitably, these reflections feed into thinking about theological education, which is increasingly being seen in technocratic terms – for example, acquiring pastoral and homiletic skills, being inducted into the corporate culture of denominations and being taught pre-packaged theological conclusions. However, we also need mentoring in the art of seeing things from a theological perspective and help in developing this skill. Theological education should be about discovering the landscape of faith, learning from those who have been there before us and personally assimilating their wisdom into our own vision.

Christians naturally come to understand experience in different ways, with important consequences for the age-old human quest to find our heart's desire. This is what we'll explore next.

The heart's desire: finding fulfilment

Although many theologians of the sixteenth and seventeenth centuries – such as Martin Luther – considered experience to be theologically significant, when I began to study theology the dominant view of the period was that engaging with experience involved an unacceptable lapse into subjectivism. Happily, some writers of that period were challenging this consensus – most notably the German theologian Gerhard Ebeling (1912–2001). In 1974, Ebeling delivered an influential lecture complaining about the 'experiential deficit in theology', in which he proposed a reconnection between theology and experience,[31] thus linking some core elements of Karl Popper's 'three worlds' that all human beings inhabit (p. 57).

So what happens when theology engages with human experience, such as our sense of deep longing for what seems to lie far beyond our reach? For writers such as Augustine and C. S. Lewis, to rightly understand such an experience is the first step towards encountering what it points to. In the final section of this chapter, we'll delve into this theme by looking at the idea of the fulfilment of our heart's desire.

Early Christian writers explored the idea that Christianity satisfied human longings and aspirations at three levels. First, it brought to fulfilment the hopes and longings of Judaism, from which Christianity originally emerged. Christ's declaration in the Sermon on the Mount was widely seen as a manifesto of this position: 'Do not think that I have come to abolish the Law or the Prophets; I have not come to abolish them but to fulfil them' (Matt. 5.17).

Christianity's relationship with Judaism gradually came to be seen as of diminishing relevance as Christianity rapidly established itself in Roman and Greek culture in the late first century. Many regarded Christianity as the fulfilment of the classic human quest for wisdom, highlighting the way that it seemed to fulfil some important themes in the writings of philosophers such as Plato and Plotinus.

Other early Christian writers, however, located the significance of Christianity at a more existential level. The Oxford philosopher Iris Murdoch reflected on the human experience of longing in an imagined dialogue between the Greek philosophers Plato and Socrates. How are we to make sense of a deep sense of yearning that nothing seems able to quench? She notes two answers:

> PLATO: Our home is elsewhere, and it draws us like a magnet.
> SOCRATES: Our home may be elsewhere, but we are condemned to exile, to live here with our fellow exiles.[32]

Some found this Platonic framework helpful in exploring the notion that there is a created homing instinct within us. This instinct may not be able to get us home on its own, but it reassures us that there is one to be found and points us in the right direction.

For Augustine of Hippo, Christianity offered a vision of a God who was able to fulfil the deepest longings of the human heart. This is expressed in his famous prayer: 'You have made us for yourself, and our heart is restless until it finds its rest in you.'[33] The human experience of longing needs to be interpreted *theologically* to understand what it really means and what it points towards. For Augustine, human beings have some inbuilt longing to relate to God (an idea often expressed in terms of bearing the 'image of God'), so that finding and embracing God is about becoming what we are *meant to be* and attaining joy and peace in doing so. Augustine sets the idea of the 'restless human heart' in search of God alongside that of a God who comes in search of us, entering into history to encounter and transform us.

Yet Augustine warns us that we often seem to be drawn to things that fall short of our true goals, causing us to be disappointed, if not disillusioned. Rowan Williams, one of the most perceptive of the contemporary interpreters of Augustine, suggests that attempts to find peace, authenticity and happiness on our own terms and in our own strength will simply end in tears:

> We are frustrated and disappointed in what we try to satisfy ourselves with and we create idols and fantasies to save ourselves from emptiness, and so deepen our bondage and anger and misery (it is like drinking sea water to quench our thirst).[34]

For Augustine, only God is able to satisfy the deepest longings of the human heart, for the simple reason that this is the end for which we were created.

In this chapter, I've tried to show how Christian theology gives us a viewpoint, a way of seeing reality, that allows us to discern – not invent! – meaning and value. These are not qualities that we can read off the world, like the colour of the leaves in our garden or the temperature of the air around us. They are created by a world view, a larger picture of our world that enables us to *interpret*, and not merely observe, our world.

As we saw when reflecting on the work of the philosopher Charles Taylor (pp. 18–21), some people try to adopt a neutral view of the world that doesn't rest on any larger vision of reality. Yet, as Taylor notes perceptively, this means that questions about 'what is good, or worthwhile, or admirable, or of value' simply cannot be answered. Why not? Because both meaning and value are *interpretations* of reality. They result from looking at life through a philosophical or theological lens.

As I've stressed throughout, Christianity locates us within a big picture so that we can position ourselves within our complex world. Or, to put it another way, Christianity tells us who we are by inviting us to work out how we fit into this larger scheme of things. We have to learn to see ourselves as standing within this big picture, and to discern how this helps to make sense of our world and our place, significance and value within it.

6

Wonder: expanding our vision of life

Studying theology sustains our sense of wonder. It creates in us a desire to explore and understand things better, partly by intimating how much more there is to discover. An experience of wonder 'momentarily suspends habitual ways of looking at the world and instead lures people into new and creative engagement with their surroundings.'[1] It makes us receptive to rethinking and reimagining the life of faith.

Of course, we don't experience this sense of wonder on our own; others help us to share in their experience and, thus, enrich ours. Michael Mayne (1929–2006), a former dean of Westminster Abbey in London, is one of many to note the importance of individuals such as theologians and poets in helping us to expand our sense of wonder. He encourages his readers to 'listen with your full attention to those who, as it were, touch your sleeve and invite you to see what the landscape and the journey look like to them. And most especially those who have a reverend and infectious wonder.'[2]

Mayne's advice is to be taken seriously. I remember my sense of delight, a year after I first began to study theology, in reading some words by Karl Barth in which he described the intellectual excitement of being a theologian. Eberhard Busch's biography of Barth had just appeared in English translation and provided an account of a lecture Barth gave in Paris in April 1934, setting out his vision of theology:

> Of all disciplines, theology is the fairest, the one that moves the head and heart most fully, the one that comes closest to human reality, the one that gives the clearest perspective on the truth which every discipline seeks. It is a landscape like of those of Umbria and Tuscany with views which are distant and yet clear.[3]

Like any good theologian, Barth acted as a signpost pointing to what he had discovered in the hope that others might find it as well. Barth 'touched my sleeve' and showed me what the theological landscape and journey looked like, and *felt* like, to him. I shared, and still share, his sense of wonder at the intellectual and imaginative scope of theology, expressed in his hope that the theologian's work should be wholly governed by a 'logic of wonder'.

Barth's image of theology as a rich landscape helps us to grasp that investigating its many features expands our vision of the world. In his *The Colossus of Maroussi* (1941), Henry Miller, too, offers a lyrical account of how exploring the wild landscape of Greece on the eve of the Second World War challenged his 'false, restricted life' and opened up a new appreciation of the world and his place within it: 'The light of Greece opened my eyes, penetrated my pores, expanded my whole being.'[4] That's what happened to me as I explored the landscape of my new faith, hanging out with fellow travellers from the past and present and absorbing their wisdom.

Theology engages our minds, hearts and imaginations. It helps us to make sense of our world and our lives. It engages with the great questions of human happiness and wellbeing and it allows us to *see* reality in a new way. Theology is about stepping into an overarching narrative and finding our place within this grand story – not one that we have invented but one we have discovered along with others before us, who can enrich our own vision from their experience and reflections.

Why wonder matters

Wonder creates a gateway into a multilayered understanding of our world, causing us to look at it with sustained attention as we realize it possesses greater depth than we realized. Many know the feeling of being in the presence of something vast that transcends their understanding and hints at something beyond the horizons of their knowledge. Philosophy, religion and science can all be traced back to an experience of wonder that opened our minds and hearts to explore new territories and ask fresh questions.

I know scientists who believe that their calling came from an overwhelming experience of awe in the solemn stillness of a night sky or a sense of astonishment at the diversity of life forms in the oceans. Something similar happened to me back in the early 1960s. Over a period of several nights, I had looked through a telescope at the moons of Jupiter slowly rotating around the giant planet. I had seen the fuzzy patches of light that I knew were distant galaxies far beyond our own. And I wanted to know more, to go deeper into the fabric of this astonishing universe into which I found myself thrown. So I decided that I would become a scientist.

Studying Albert Einstein during my first year as a chemistry undergraduate opened my eyes to the remarkable ability of quantum theory to make sense of our world. Einstein spoke of a sense of 'rapturous amazement'[5] at being able to identify the laws of nature that governed the cosmos. Yet Einstein was also clear that we could never fully perceive the immensity of our universe. What little we can observe points to a far greater unseen reality that lies beyond our capacity to grasp and hold.

Einstein highlights the point we noted earlier: that a sense of wonder at the universe often leads to a desire to study it and appreciate it in greater depth. It is as if this sense of wonder or amazement expands our minds, making us receptive to more profound ways of understanding things. Psychologists such as Dacher Keltner (b. 1962) tell us that the experience of awe or wonder is good for us. It directs our attention away from our own preoccupations, it helps us to realize that we are part of something greater than ourselves and it makes us more generous towards others.[6] A sense of wonder opens us up to new intellectual possibilities as we realize the limiting effect of mere theories.

The same goes for theology. I know theologians whose intellectual journeys were triggered by a sense of wonder, evoked by worship, which seemed to point to a greater reality than they had yet encountered. Grasping the beauty of God, or the intellectual richness of Christianity, makes us want to understand God and the Christian faith better. A primal desire for God sets off a cascade of related longings, including a yearning to understand more *about* God. It's a great motivation for the study of theology!

Back in the eleventh century, Anselm of Canterbury coined a phrase that expresses this point neatly: '*fides quaerens intellectum* (faith seeking understanding)'. The nature of faith is such that it wants to go deeper and understand what is believed. Knowing God leads to a desire to know more about

God, to expand our vision of God both intellectually and imaginatively. We want, to use a phrase from C. S. Lewis, to go 'further up and further in'[7] to the Christian landscape.

Yet the link between wonder and theology is more complex than this suggests. It is certainly true that many find an experience of religious wonder to be intellectually transformative, in that it calls into question the adequacy of existing ways of thinking. An expanded vision of reality can thus arise. Yet this same expanded vision of reality can help sustain a sense of wonder over time, partly by helping us to understand it and recapture its significance. T. S. Eliot is one of many to point out that we can have an experience but fail to see its meaning. Theology gives us a framework to understand the meaning of what we experience. C. S. Lewis, for example, interprets the human experience of yearning for fulfilment as our intuitive realization of the basic human need for God, who alone can satisfy our deepest desires.

Attentiveness: seeing and respecting nature as God's creation

In his reflections on the 'Brave New World' of modern Western culture, Aldous Huxley (1894–1963) suggested that human beings have an 'almost infinite appetite for distractions.'[8] Maybe that's why the spiritual writer Thomas Merton (1915–68) tells us that we need to refocus, to find out how we can liberate ourselves from captivity to the world around us through a 'quieting and ordering' so that God can 'find us' and 'take possession of us'.[9] We are indebted to the French spiritual philosopher Simone Weil for one of the most insightful discussions of the proper cultivation of attentiveness towards God.

Weil's best-known work is *Attente de Dieu* (1950), traditionally translated into English as 'Waiting for God'. The French original, however, is better translated as 'Attentiveness towards God'. Weil's concern is about becoming receptive and open to the truth: 'Attention consists of suspending our thought, leaving it detached, empty, and ready to be penetrated by the object.'[10] It is a readiness to receive, an anticipation of the advent of truth, a sense of expectation of encounter with something worthwhile and potentially enriching and transformative.

Weil's discussion of attentiveness, however, is not primarily practical. It's not as if she intended to provide a list of helpful tips for self-improvement. For Weil, attentiveness must be recognized as a moral, even theological, obligation. Attentiveness towards God is a recognition of our emptiness and our inability to be self-sufficient. We look towards God with a sense of hope and anticipation because God is both the enabler and the goal of our quest for meaning and truth.

Let's turn from what might seem to be abstract theological reflection to a direct engagement with the beauty of nature informed by a theological lens: the doctrine of creation. It's long been recognized that creation is a pointer to the Creator, a visible and tangible expression of the nature of God. The seventh-century Byzantine theologian Maximus the Confessor (*c.*580–662) was well aware of this interplay between theology and the contemplation of nature:

> So the soul flees toward the intellectual contemplation of nature, as to the inside of a Church and to a place of peaceful sanctuary . . . And there it learns to recognize the essential meanings of things as if through the readings from Holy Scripture.[11]

The medieval theologian Bonaventure of Bagnoregio (1221–74) followed in the tradition of Francis of Assisi by regarding the created order as 'as a means of self-revelation so that, like a mirror of God or a divine footprint, it might lead us to love and praise our Creator.'[12] It is usual for Christians to become attentive to the vastness and intricacy of the natural world in the belief and expectation that it might help us to grasp at least something of the beauty and glory of God.

The patient, respectful and disciplined attentiveness towards nature commended by Bonaventure is neatly expressed by Henry Miller: 'The moment one gives close attention to any thing, even a blade of grass it becomes a mysterious, awesome, indescribably magnificent world in itself.'[13] The English poet Thomas Traherne (1636–74) offers us perhaps one of the finest examples of a theologically attentive reading of the natural world.[14] Traherne anticipates Miller's attentiveness to its intricacy yet makes explicit theological connections that go far beyond a surface reading of natural diversity and complexity:

> You never Enjoy the World aright, till you see how a Sand exhibiteth the Wisdom and Power of God: And Prize in evry thing the Service which they do you, by Manifesting His Glory and Goodness to your Soul, far more than the Visible Beauty on their Surface, or the Material Services, they can do your Body.[15]

As Traherne and other theologically informed poets such as Gerard Manley Hopkins point out, it is not enough to appreciate the beauty of nature or the benefits that the natural world can provide for human comfort and survival; we need to go beyond and beneath a surface reading of nature and study it as a set of signs pointing to God and illuminating the human situation. Theology provides us with a key for interpreting those signs.

Michael Mayne is particularly interesting on this. He wrote of his sense of wonder in the presence of nature while spending a month living amidst the stunning landscape of the Swiss Alps:

> My subject is wonder, and my starting point is so obvious it often escapes us. It is me, sitting at a table looking out on the world. It is the fact that I exist, that there is anything at all. It is the *givenness* that astonishes: the fact that the mountains, the larch tree, the gentian, the jay, *exist*, and that someone called *me* is here to observe them.[16]

Mayne's reflections on the astonishing reality of individual human existence models a theologically informed attentiveness to the natural world that allows us to discern its details and depths. When properly used, theology renders the natural world transparent to the divine and thus allows us to see what really matters in life.[17]

The way that we see something also determines how we value it. Theology gives us a lens to view the natural world not as an object for exploitation but as God's creation, which has been entrusted to us for safekeeping. Once the natural order is perceived in this way, we realize the ethical imperative of caring for the creation not simply to ensure the future of humanity but also because we are *responsible* for it.

The intellectual appeal of faith

Earlier in this chapter, I explored the importance of wonder and awe in human life, drawing on the work of the psychologist Dacher Keltner. In identifying what he calls the 'elicitors' of awe, Keltner pointed to evidence that this could include an experience of God, a grand vista, and 'the breadth and scope of a grand theory'.[18] As I discovered for myself, the conceptual capaciousness of such a 'grand theory' or 'big picture' draws us in to explore it and holds us once we have embraced it.

We need to experience this sense of wonder at the scope of Christian theology. I learned it through reading Barth. There are others who can help us – such as G. K. Chesterton, C. S. Lewis, and Dorothy L. Sayers. When lecturing on theology at Oxford, I often reflected on Christ's summary of the first commandment: 'Love the Lord your God with all your heart and with all your soul and with all your mind and with all your strength' (Mark 12.30). Every faculty we possess is caught up in the process of loving God and being transformed by this encounter and experience. This transformation extends to the human mind (Rom. 12.2) as its vision is enlarged by grace to accommodate more of the vast reality of God.

Like many teenagers growing up in the late 1960s, I found myself attracted, as I mentioned earlier, to the intellectual vision of Marxism. There were several reasons for this. For a start, it placed me – or so I thought back then – on the right side of history. It set out a series of social and political goals that I admired then. But Marxism was not a smorgasbord of disconnected ideas; it offered a coherent world view that integrated these ideas within a grander vision of the world.

Once you stepped inside this big picture, its specific values and goals followed naturally.

The Marxist thinker I came to admire most – and still read today – was the Italian writer Antonio Gramsci (1891–1937), who made a distinction between those who were drawn to Marxism because of its social and political agendas and those who were attracted to it on account of its intellectual appeal. For Gramsci, there was a danger that Marxism would lose touch with intellectuals and simply become a political movement defined by allegiance to the Communist Party of the Soviet Union.[19]

For Gramsci, Marxist beliefs and values are grounded in and sustained by the Marxist 'grand theory' or big picture. Many embrace this vision of reality because they find it intellectually compelling and imaginatively exciting. I have experienced the magnetism of its appeal myself![20] Perhaps more importantly, I now know many others who have been drawn to Christianity for the same reason. One of the roles of theology is to articulate the Christian grand theory so that its luminous intellectual and imaginative vision can be seen and appreciated. Theology aims to help us to love God with all our minds.

Yet Gramsci makes a further point that is important theologically: the category of 'intellectuals' extends far beyond the academy. Gramsci points to individuals who were embedded in the wider social fabric who could grasp and interpret Marxist ideas and apply them to their political and social situations. Politicians, journalists, trade unionists and peasants all played an important intellectual role in reshaping public thinking along Marxist lines and in interpreting and applying ideas to wider society. These 'organic intellectuals', to use Gramsci's term, were rooted in culture, capable of grasping the Marxist vision and applying it to their local situations.[21]

Many early Christian writers were 'organic theologians', to adapt Gramsci's term, in that they could see how the Christian gospel was to be interpreted and applied to their congregations. They wrote and reflected from within the community of faith – not from *above* it and certainly not from *outside* it. The rise of universities may have created a new style of academic theology, yet this development does not in any way detract from the importance of the 'organic theology' that was characteristic of this early period in Christian history. In fact, it continues to this day and remains important and influential, even if it is not widely known by this name.

Parish clergy function as organic theologians through their preaching, helping to sustain a sense of identity and significance within their congregations. So do popular Christian writers, such as G. K. Chesterton, Dorothy L. Sayers and Marilynne Robinson, who are able to interpret Christian ideas and express them in the language of their communities of readers. The many Christian websites and blogs devoted to theological questions also fall into this category. 'Organic theologians' can articulate the importance of theology in sustaining Christian identity and confidence within their communities in the face of alternative cultural narratives.

Gramsci's view of 'organic intellectuals' in no way detracts from the importance of theology; rather, it increases its reach and encourages local implementations and translations. Nor does it set up a tension between 'academic' and 'organic' theologians; instead, it recognizes their different spheres of operations and the different skills these require. In my view, 'organic theologians' hold the key to the future of the Christian community in many parts of the world. They need to be encouraged and resourced by their academic colleagues. Without them, Christianity may well be reduced to bland, generic pastoral and spiritual practices that lack the resilience and depth that is so clearly needed to confront the uncertainties of the future.

We need intellectuals, whether academic or 'organic', to exercise a prophetic role within the Church and our wider culture by naming what is wrong and what needs to be done. In the dying years of the Weimar Republic, the sociologist Karl Mannheim argued that a new type of person had emerged 'whose special task is to provide an interpretation of the world', and to 'play the part of watchmen in what otherwise would be a pitch-black night'. For Mannheim, that is what intellectuals were meant to be and do: offer a prophetic interpretation and critique of our world from the perspective of what he called 'a certain "world-postulate"'.[22] And some of these prophetic intellectuals have been Christians, such as W. H. Auden and Dorothy L. Sayers, whose deep immersion in the Christian theological tradition enabled them to see the world as it really was and demand its reform and renewal.

Speaking about God: preserving the mystery

The term 'mystery' is widely used to refer to something that cannot be fully grasped by human reason. Albert Einstein insisted that a sense of 'the mysterious' was the source of all true art and science, just as an 'experience of mysteriousness' lay at the heart of religion. 'What I see in nature is a magnificent structure that we can only grasp imperfectly.'[23] This 'inability of the human mind to understand deeply the harmony of the Universe',[24] Einstein argued, meant that we cannot hope to provide a full account of the vast and complex cosmic reality. The quantum theorist Werner Heisenberg (1901–76), similarly, insisted that scientific thinking 'always hovers over a bottomless depth' and had to come to terms with the 'impenetrable darkness that lies behind the ideas language is able to express.'[25]

Theologians also use the term 'mystery', understanding this to refer not to something that is irrational but to something that lies tantalizingly beyond the reach of what human reason can fully grasp. In the end, our minds just aren't big enough to cope with the conceptual vastness of God so brilliantly expressed in the theological notion of 'glory'. God simply overwhelms our mental capacities.

The Franciscan theologian Thomas Weinandy (b. 1946) uses a nice turn of phrase: 'Because God, who can never be fully comprehended, lies at the heart of all theological enquiry, theology by its nature is not a problem solving enterprise but rather a mystery discerning enterprise.'[26] The danger is that we try to reduce everything to what the human mind can cope with instead of trying to expand our intellectual vision to take in these larger realities despite the mental discomfort they may cause.

In one sense, theology aims to preserve the mystery of God not by shutting down discussion about God but, rather, through recognizing that discussion can never hope to do intellectual justice to the glory of God. The temptation is either to focus on what we can grasp and hope that the rest is unimportant or to reduce this grand vision to what our minds can accommodate. Since both these strategies distort, disfigure and mislead, theology is forced to occupy the middle ground between them and learn to live with this tension. Theology thus tries to make rational sense of mystery while realizing that a mystery cannot be fully rationalized!

This dilemma has long been recognized in Christian theology. Hilary of Poitiers (*c.*310–*c.*367) – a bishop who is widely considered to be one of the two most important Latin-speaking theologians of the fourth century (the other being Ambrose of Milan (*c.*339–397)) – noted that 'we must place the poor resources of our language under strain to express thoughts that are too great for words.'[27] As Thomas Aquinas discovered, our words simply break under the strain of trying to describe the glory and majesty of God.

On 6 December 1273, Aquinas abruptly stopped writing his massive *Summa Theologiae* ('The Totality of Theology'). His secretary, Reginald of Piperno, was puzzled and asked for an explanation. Aquinas replied that he had been overwhelmed by a vision of God that simply could not be conceptualized: 'Everything that I have written seems like chaff (*palea*) to me compared to those things that I have seen and that have been revealed to me.'[28] His theological writings were not wrong; he was simply silenced by his realization that they were totally incapable of doing justice to God.

Christian theology does not see the concept of mystery as a *problem*. Why not? Because the concept of mystery points to the imaginative vastness and spiritual inexhaustibility of God. There is always more to appreciate about God. That's why the best theology leads naturally into prayer and worship as we catch a glimpse of the glory of this God, perhaps sharing something of Aquinas's sense of being overwhelmed by a glory that so vastly exceeds our capacity to express it in words.

The failed quest for certainty: Tomáš Halík on faith and mystery

One of the theologians I have come to respect most in recent years is the Czech writer Tomáš Halík (b. 1948), who established himself as a winsome and gracious theological voice following the collapse of communism throughout eastern Europe, particularly the 'Velvet Revolution' in Prague during 1989. Halík had been active in underground Catholic circles throughout the period of Marxist rule and played a significant role in giving theological direction to the Czech church in the post-revolutionary world.

In Halík's view, both secular culture and many within the Church have been deluded by quick intellectual fixes and false certainties. He sees faith not as a cast-iron set of certainties but as 'a journey, a way of seeking, a way into the depths of meaning'.[29] The Christian God is a 'pilgrim God', who cannot be captured with conceptual precision by our intellectual systems and traditions but, rather, is to be discovered as a living, meaning-creating presence as we journey through uncertainty. This leads Halík to emphasize that faith is what draws us into 'the Mystery that is called God.'[30]

Halík is critical of the overconfident assertions made by atheists, religious fundamentalists and enthusiasts of a superficial and facile faith. All, he suggests, 'run roughshod over the mystery we call God'.[31] A mystery is inexhaustible, something that no single theological generation can fully grasp even if they can pass on to us their hard-won insights. It is by journeying with God through an unknown and bewildering landscape that we break free from past limiting notions of God or the gospel, which have led us to enclose the living God within the confines of our concepts and traditions.

Halík notes that many of the great theological and spiritual writers of the past found themselves facing uncertainty and change as an old order seemed to be giving way to an indeterminate and unpredictable future in which the trusted certainties of the past might no longer be valid. What kept them going, Halík suggests, is a deep intuitive belief that God would prove able to meet the challenges of this new situation. That, he suggests, is why the 'first and last sentence of any theology' should be 'God is mystery'.[32]

To sum up, then, faith is not assent to a limited rational account of God but, rather, involves a commitment to a journey of exploration in which the immensity and inexhaustibility of God are experienced and uncovered along the road as we find ourselves facing new situations and challenges. The task of theology is to uncover how the disclosure of this inexhaustible mystery in the Bible, and the long history of Christian reflection on the biblical text, may help us to engage with new questions and cope with new situations. Precisely because God is inexhaustible, no one individual theologian or even generation of theologians can hope to fully grasp the wonder of God. There is always more to discover and experience.

The Trinity: wrestling with mystery

Critics of theology often point to the doctrine of the Trinity as a piece of theological gibberish that the Church could well do without. Who can take such logical and mathematical nonsense seriously? It's just a speculative complexity imposed upon the simple language of the New Testament. Not only is it incomprehensible, it doesn't *do* anything other than cause Christians intellectual embarrassment. Why not limit ourselves to the simple vocabulary of the New Testament?

Disconcertingly, the 'simple' language about God that we find in the New Testament turns out, on closer inspection, to be rather more complicated than it seems. The New Testament epistles show an entanglement between the identity and functions of God, Christ and the Holy Spirit. Theological reflection did not create this complexity; rather, it aims to *preserve* it and *express* it as reliably as possible – even if, as Hilary of Poitiers points out, this involves going beyond the vocabulary of the New Testament. For Hilary, to fully understand what we believe and to defend this against misunderstanding, we need 'to speak about God by going beyond what God determined beforehand'.[33] While the Trinitarian language of the Church is not explicitly present in the New Testament, Christians found it necessary to develop this in order to express and hold together its rich implicit account of the nature and activity of God.

It is widely agreed that the revival of theological confidence in the Christian doctrine of the Trinity is mainly due to two twentieth-century theologians: the Swiss Protestant Karl Barth and the German Catholic Karl Rahner. Barth, for example, insists that the doctrine is the Christian Church's legitimate and necessary attempt to 'translate and exegete' the New Testament in order to set out this rich and glorious vision of the identity and character of the Christian God.[34]

Yet the simple fact is that most Christians see the doctrine of the Trinity negatively, as a rational problem, rather than positively, as a vision of God. Clergy, when called to preach on the Trinity, suddenly become amateur physicists with a fascination for the 'triple point' of water: the temperature and pressure at which its three potential forms – ice, liquid water and steam – can coexist. What conceivable relevance has this for understanding why Christians have seen the Trinity as central to their thinking about God? (None at all – except that it shows there are examples of 'three in one' in the natural world too.) Christians can hardly grow in their faith if their preachers feed them this facile nonsense. Rather, the task of preachers is to set out the glorious vision of who God is and what God does, which is expressed and enfolded by the doctrine of the Trinity, so that their congregations can grasp this vision.

Let's keep considering the relevance of this complex doctrine. For one thing, it safeguards the distinctively Christian vision of God from being confused with, or reduced to, its intellectually and imaginatively deficient rivals, such as Deism, which portrays God as an absentee creator who has no further interest in or concern for creation – a cosmic clockmaker, who has created the world, wound it up and then left it to function unattended.

Emil Brunner, a Swiss Protestant theologian who had a somewhat complicated relationship with Karl Barth, argues that the doctrine of the Trinity is essentially a 'defensive doctrine (*Schutzlehre*)',[35] designed to safeguard the Christian vision of God from reduction to its pagan or idealist counterparts. It is not something that ought itself to be preached but, rather, offers a framework within which authentic Christian preaching can take place.

A similar point was made by Catherine Mowry LaCugna (1952–97), an American Catholic theologian based at the

University of Notre Dame, who based her account of the Trinity on the work of Karl Rahner. For LaCugna, all learning about the mystery of God is actually a matter of unlearning, of leaving behind preconceived ideas and predetermined ideas of God that we have absorbed from our intellectual and cultural contexts, in order that we may grasp God *properly*, both intellectually and relationally. The doctrine of the Trinity is the specifically Christian way of speaking about God, which 'summarizes what it means to participate in the life of God through Jesus Christ in the Spirit'.[36]

LaCugna then makes the point that so many preachers fail to draw out, namely the spiritual benefits that this doctrine brings:

> The purpose of the doctrine of the Trinity is not to diagnose why God is the way God is, but to remind us to 'taste and see the goodness of God' revealed in creation, Christ, and communion with one another in the Spirit.[37]

For LaCugna, the doctrine has both an objective and subjective payload. It enables us to grasp the glory of God and experience God's goodness in and through a *relationship* with God. Augustine of Hippo made a similar point: 'Nothing can exceed the fulness of our happiness, which is to enjoy God the Trinity in whose image we are created.'[38]

Another expression of this vision of the Trinitarian God is found in the *Lorica*, the hymn often known as 'St Patrick's Breastplate' traditionally ascribed to Patrick, patron saint of Ireland. I feel a special affinity with this approach, as I was baptized at the cathedral built beside Patrick's grave in Downpatrick (the Gaelic name *Dún Pádraig* means 'Patrick's stronghold'). In the hymn, Patrick surveys the work of God in creation and redemption, affirming that the 'strong name' of this God can be relied upon to enfold and protect the believer.

The poem evokes a sense of wonder at the vastness of nature and the fine details of Christ's work of redemption, before claiming the power of this God in the midst of the perils and uncertainties of life. The Trinity names the 'strong God', who can be trusted in times of danger and doubt. For Patrick, the Trinity is not to be seen as a specious piece of theological speculation but as an attempt to express the fullness of God's nature and being, particularly the impact this compelling vision of God has on the challenges of life.

These lines of thought clearly point towards a link between theology, worship and prayer, which needs further exploration.

Glimpsing glory: theology, worship and spirituality

Intellectual historians often express concern about the fragmentation of human knowledge disintegrating into specialist realms. For instance, what Isaac Newton knew simply as 'natural philosophy' has broken down into physics, chemistry, biology, astronomy and a myriad of other disconnected scientific disciplines, each of which has become so specialized that there is little dialogue or collaboration between them.[39]

Many feel that this has also happened to theology.[40] In terms of today's academic disciplines, Augustine of Hippo was an apologist, a practical theologian, a philosopher of religion, a systematic theologian and a New Testament scholar. But Augustine saw himself simply as a *theologian*, seamlessly weaving together the many elements of his vision of loving God with all his mind.

Theology and spirituality are now widely regarded as separate disciplines and practices yet, for most Christian writers down the ages, theology and spirituality might be helpfully *distinguished*, but certainly not meaningfully *separated*. Christian theologians have always believed theology and spirituality incapable of being separated without a violation of their integrity. For example, Puritanism was a movement in England and North America that recognized an integral and seamless connection between doctrine and piety, and it offers a framework for those wishing to make similar connections today.[41]

The Princeton theologian Ellen Charry argues that modernity tends to think of 'truth' as the acquisition of information enabling us to control our world rather than a quest for authenticity and personal transformation: 'Knowing the truth no longer implied loving it, wanting it, and being transformed by it, because the truth no longer brings the knower to God but to use information to subdue nature.'[42] Theology, according to Charry, enfolds a vision of truth as a luminous and overwhelming vision of God that shapes spiritual practice – the disciplines and habits that help Christians to live out the values and norms of their faith. This experience of the glory of God brings perspective to our lives, helping us to abandon the conceit that we are at the centre of things.

More recent theological discussion of this point has drawn on Pierre Hadot's claim that classic Greek philosophy was not so much about discovering right ways of thinking but, rather, developing an appropriate 'way of life (*manière de vivre.*)'[43] This, Hadot (1922–2010) suggested, would be based on a set of practices that reinforced such an understanding of nature and the good life. Philosophy thus aims to help the process of personal formation that is required to live out such a mode of thinking. As we noted previously, early Christianity was seen by some observers as a 'philosophy' not in the sense of an abstract set of ideas but, rather, as a way of achieving wisdom and authenticity. A disciplined contemplation of the world leads to the development of practices and disciplines that foster human wellbeing.

This point is brought out by the Cambridge theologian Sarah Coakley (b. 1951), who notes the importance of developing theologically informed spiritual disciplines (Greek: *askēsis*). These disciplines or practices both embody theological principles and help us to achieve their application in life. Coakley, for example, notes how 'silent prayer' involves a renunciation of the notion of being in control of things, leading to a reinterpretation of the notion of 'vulnerability' and a de-centering of the self and its desires through the hope of a mystical union with God:

> The 'paradox of power and vulnerability' is, I believe, uniquely focused in this act of silent waiting on the divine in prayer. This is because we can only be properly 'empowered' here if we cease to set the agenda, if we 'make space' for God to be God.[44]

Coakley and others make it clear that there is a natural and essential link between theology and spirituality – between the two enterprises that the evangelical theologian J. I. Packer termed 'knowing about God' and 'knowing God',[45] or what Lewis referred to as 'intellectual assent' and 'imaginative enjoyment.'[46] These two practices may be distinguished. They cannot, however, be separated.

Why is this important? Because it reinforces a central theme of this short book: namely, that theology and the life of faith are inseparable. Theology enfolds and informs the Christian life, establishing its foundation and its goal, while reassuring us that God does not leave us on our own as we try to become better people, but accompanies and refreshes us as we journey.

7

Conclusion: making theology matter

What's the point of theology? This short book has sketched some answers to this entirely proper and reasonable question. Yet perhaps the most important is this: theology matters because *Christianity* matters and theology aims to preserve, express and convey its essence. If Christianity is like a pearl 'of great value' (Matt. 13.45–6), theology tries to describe that pearl, putting into words what is so special about it, how it may be found and the difference that finding and possessing it makes to someone's life. It is impossible to read the New Testament epistles or the sermons of early Christian writers without a sense that something new, exciting and transformative has taken place in and through Christ, opening up a fresh and satisfying understanding of ourselves and the world.

Theology is the Christian community's attempt to imagine, describe and analyse this new world in order to enable believers to grow into and flourish within their faith, and others to gain a sense of what Christianity is all about. The Church has always struggled to find the right words to describe the treasure that has been entrusted to it – a treasure upon which its identity and survival depends. That's why theology emerged as a principled, imaginative and utterly necessary attempt to find the best ways of describing, communicating and commending this pearl of great price.

Without it, Christianity collapses, leaving only an institutional husk. Theology aims to preserve what is so special about the pearl, exhibit its beauty and explain its significance. Yes, churches need guidance on how to manage congregations, communicate effectively and use the latest technology properly. But these are supplementary and subsidiary to the matter of having something to *say* and to *show* that cannot be had elsewhere. Like it or not, theology both preserves the identity-giving vision on which the life and existence of the Church depends and offers a tried-and-tested toolkit for explaining and commending it.

So am I suggesting that all Christians should study theology? No, I am actually proposing something more radical. All Christians are theologians already, in that they think and talk about their faith. My suggestion is not that we all take up some peculiar and unnecessary hobby but that we have the courage to think more deeply about what we believe in the company of others who have done so before us.

Yes, times change. But past wisdom can be put to fresh use. To read Sohrab Ahmari's *The Unbroken Thread* (2021) is both to catch a glimpse of the potential of past wisdom to enrich and give stability in the present and to grasp the potential of writers such as Augustine, Aquinas and C. S. Lewis to illuminate contemporary political and cultural concerns.[1] Ahmari's analysis points to the importance of being rooted in something deeper than the technocratic modern world can offer. He also helps us to grasp the importance of theological education as an immersion in this tradition of wisdom, if we are to avoid the shallowness and superficiality of so many forms of contemporary religion.

On theological education

What might these reflections suggest about theological education, especially in resourcing and equipping future ministers and pastors? It's not enough to explain what Christians believe and why they believe. Rather than look *at* Christian doctrines, we need to look *through* them (George Herbert) or look *along* them (C. S. Lewis). Theology gives us a window through which we can see ourselves and the world in a new light and then live accordingly. William James (1842–1910) spoke of how religious faith often leads to 'a transfiguration of the face of nature' in which a 'new heaven seems to shine on a new earth.'[2]

Theological education is partly about helping people to *use* theology, to see their worlds and lives transfigured through its lens. They need to learn how to do this from those who, over a lifetime, have worked out how to connect theology with the life of faith in a handing down of wisdom from one generation to another. This wisdom is not simply about *understanding*, for example, Augustine, Aquinas or Barth; it is about learning *from* these theologians.

Earlier (p. 127), I noted Pierre Hadot's point about the interconnection of theory and practice in classical philosophy. What we believe about the world leads to the development of practices that both express this faith and enable it to be deepened. Too often, theological education fails to make the connection between theology, worship and spirituality, often treating these as unrelated and disconnected compartments of religious life. Yet worship, the devotional reading of Scripture and prayer are more than just a natural and proper expression of faith; they are the means by which that faith is sustained and deepened in the lives of individual believers.[3]

There is a need for churches to recover the lost art of catechesis in order to help Christians to grasp the basics of their faith. I'm not suggesting the rote learning of catechisms; rather, that we explain not merely what Christians believe but also the difference that this makes to the way we think and live.

Theology and the life of faith

Earlier, I drew on John Mackay's famous comparison of the balcony and the road, pointing out how the best theology is forged as Christians develop ways of dealing with difficult questions and situations that they encounter and then pass these on to those who follow. Augustine of Hippo was able to articulate the intellectual, moral, political and spiritual vision of the Christian faith in the early fifth century as the Roman empire, which set the framework of the established order for a millennium, began to fall to pieces around him. Like other reflective practitioners, he was able to make connections between the rich Christian big picture and his own situation.

As James K. A. Smith's *On the Road with Saint Augustine* (2019) makes clear, Augustine is a stimulating travelling companion for us today, shining light on the multiple turnings and dilemmas of the life of faith.[4] Smith's engagement with Augustine takes the form of a critical retrieval – a respectful wrestling with a wise figure from the past, aimed at understanding a new situation or problem. He looks to a thinker embedded in a specific time and place and quarries insights and wisdom that he then applies to the life of faith today. Smith asks what can be learned *from* rather than just what can be learned *about*, Augustine. Augustine thus emerges as a contemporary mentor, not a distant figure from a forgotten past of interest only to historians. And, happily, there are many others from whom we can gain wisdom.

Smith is not distorting Augustine in asking such questions, nor in adopting such an approach. I would go so far as to say that the best theology is about learning whatever we can from the great figures of both the theological past and present, not simply concerning how we think about our faith but also how we live it out in the world.[5] How does reading this theologian help me to explain my faith to others, to maintain hope in a puzzling and precarious world or to deepen my love for God and the created order that has been entrusted to us?

Theology belongs on the road, not the balcony. We can learn from those who have travelled that road before us and passed their acquired wisdom down. But we also need people who can unpack that wisdom for us, who themselves have put it into practice and can explain how they did so and the benefits this brought them. Thus, theological education is not about the transfer of information but the formation of wisdom through the shaping of reflective practitioners of the art of theology.

When I began to study theology at Oxford, my key question was how I could understand the ideas of, for example, the medieval theologian Anselm of Canterbury. Today, my question is different: what can such theologians teach me about how to live and think in a Christian way? I want to learn *from* these people, not just learn *about* them. They are the teachers and I am the student. Anselm, after all, is remembered for both his works of theology and his prayers and meditations.[6] He saw no disconnection between these fields and neither should we. That's why preaching is so important: it is an attempt to connect up the core vision at the heart of the Christian faith with the concerns, needs and hopes of a local community of faith. Preachers are the interpreters of this rich tradition, able to make the connections that will sustain the life of faith for those who hear them.

What's the point of theology?

So what *is* the point of theology? Let me close by making three suggestions and exploring them briefly. Theology explains what Christianity is all about to those beyond the churches; it enables individual Christian believers to deepen their faith and understanding; and it enables the churches to be refreshed, renewed and challenged continually by the vision of reality that brought them into being in the first place.

First, theology has a public function, in that it aims to explain what Christians believe, why Christians believe these ideas might be right and the difference that these ideas make. In this role, theology is *informative*, helping to reveal the vision that lies behind Christian poetry, art and literature. There is no expectation that a public audience will *agree* with these ideas, but there is a reasonable expectation that this audience will take the community of faith's own account of its beliefs seriously.

This is not an unreasonable claim for cultural privilege; it is simply a statement of the general principle that we ought to be attentive to others' views and do our best to understand them and not to misrepresent them. That's why conversations across boundaries are so important, particularly in debunking some popular misconceptions and misrepresentations – such as the clichés that abound in the writings of New Atheist polemicists, which actually embarrass intelligent and informed atheists.[7]

Second, theology is important for individual believers' lives of faith as they aim to go deeper into the vision of reality that Christianity makes possible. This expansion of our individual perceptions of the gospel can be catalysed in several ways. It happens through reading theologians as they reflect on central issues of faith (I have engaged with a representative sample of such writers throughout this book). It happens through listening to thoughtful sermons, which work the angles of Christian faith and open up helpful lines of thought. It happens when reading the Bible, often in the company of an able commentator.

To reiterate a point that I made earlier, theological engagement does not *diminish* personal faith; it has the capacity to *enrich* it through learning to love God with all our minds in conversation with others. Theology offers us an expanded understanding of Christian commonplaces. For example, instead of thinking of the church as a club, we come to see it as a community within which God's grace is active, helping us to grow in faith and holiness.

Third, theology is essential for the future of churches as institutions. It articulates the spiritual and imaginative vision that brought them into being and is the ultimate reason for their continued existence. It maps the landscape of faith in which we discover holiness, beauty and glory. The loveliness of the pearl of great value (Matt. 13.45–6) cannot be fully expressed in words, yet theology can capture our sense of wonder and astonishment in the presence of something deep and transformative that draws us to itself in ways we do not fully understand. Beauty elicits desire, creating a sense of longing for participation that goes beyond mere observation.

As Christian spiritual writers down the ages have pointed out, we are not simply drawn *towards* this vision; we are drawn *into* it, sensing that it may answer our deepest questions and satisfy our deepest longings. And once we stand inside it, we realize its ability to hold together our complex world, excite us about the new possibilities it discloses and reassure us that we matter to God. That's why a good theology will lead into apologetics, spirituality, evangelism, social engagement and pastoral care. If the leadership of churches passes to those with no sense of this theological vision, those churches are likely to become little more than repositories of generalized spiritual and moral banalities.

So what is the point of theology? I began this small book by noting that there might be no right answers to this question, before offering my own thoughts on what theology is, why it matters and why it is so satisfying. Yet there are other approaches that you might like to explore as you craft your own understanding of what theology is, how it ought to be done and the difference that it makes to life. And while other theologians might offer alternative and probably better answers than mine, we are agreed that there is indeed a point to theology. It's not going to go away.

Taking things further

This book is not a theology textbook, but it may stimulate you to want to know more about this discipline and to follow through on some of the writers that I engage with in the text. Happily, you can find an enormous amount of helpful material on theological issues and individual theologians online. However, I will mention some printed resources that may also be useful.

If you've found this book interesting, you might like two others I wrote, which are used to teach Christian theology throughout the world in colleges, seminaries and universities. Both are based on lectures that I gave at Oxford University in the 1980s and 1990s, and have been updated and expanded over the past 30 years:

Alister E. McGrath, *Christian Theology: An Introduction* 6th edn (Oxford: Wiley-Blackwell, 2016).

Alister E. McGrath, *Theology: The Basics* 4th edn (Oxford: Wiley-Blackwell, 2016).

The first is long and comprehensive; the second is shorter and easier to read. However, both are accessible.

It really helps to engage with original texts so that you can read other theologians with a sense of the approach they take and the ideas they develop. I've written two such collections of texts (or 'readings'). Each introduces the text in question and guides you through it, telling you what to look for:

Alister E. McGrath, *The Christian Theology Reader* 5th edn (Oxford: Wiley-Blackwell, 2017).

Alister E. McGrath, *Theology: The Basic Readings* 3rd edn (Oxford: Wiley-Blackwell, 2018).

Again, both these textbooks are designed to be accessible. The first is very comprehensive; the second is shorter and easier to read.

If you want to know more about my own journey as a theologian and some of the ideas that I find especially interesting, you might like to take a look at these:

Alister E. McGrath, *My Theology: Return from a Distant Country* (London: Darton, Longman & Todd, 2021).

Alister E. McGrath, *Through a Glass Darkly: Journeys through Science, Faith and Doubt* (London: Hodder & Stoughton, 2020).

I also maintain a website on which I post videos of my theological lectures and reflections: <alistermcgrath.net>. All content is free and may be copied, shared or downloaded.

Although you may find my own introductions to theology helpful, there are many other wonderful guides to the field. I recommend the following, all of which are widely used in theological education at a variety of levels:

Ellen T. Charry, *By the Renewing of Your Minds: The Pastoral Function of Christian Doctrine* (New York: Oxford University Press, 1997).

David Ford, *Theology: A Very Short Introduction* 2nd edn (Oxford: Oxford University Press, 2013).

David Ford and Rachel Muers eds, *The Modern Theologians: An Introduction to Christian Theology Since 1918* 3rd edn (Oxford: Wiley-Blackwell, 2005).

Wayne Grudem, *Systematic Theology: An Introduction to Biblical Doctrine* 2nd edn (Grand Rapids, MI: Zondervan, 1994).

Mark A. McIntosh, *Divine Teaching: An Introduction to Christian Theology* (Malden, MA: Blackwell, 2008).

Daniel L. Migliore, *Faith Seeking Understanding: An Introduction to Christian Theology* 2nd edn (Grand Rapids, MI: Eerdmans, 2004).

Roger E. Olson, *The Journey of Modern Theology: From Reconstruction to Deconstruction* (Downers Grove, IL: InterVarsity Press, 2014).

Miroslav Volf and Matthew Croasmun, *For the Life of the World: Theology that Makes a Difference* (Grand Rapids, MI: Brazos Press, 2019).

Questions for reflection

Many people find it helpful to use study questions to make sure that they've got the most out of their reading. The questions below will help you both to reflect on the approach set out in this book and develop your own.

1 Discovering theology: seeing things in a new way

1. How can we see the same thing in new ways? What difference does it make?
2. What is the distinction between seeing the world around us as 'nature' and as 'creation'?
3. How helpful do you find C. S. Lewis's idea of a 'supposal'?

2 Theology as a 'big picture'

1. What difference does thinking about Christianity as a 'big picture' make?
2. How might you summarize Dorothy L. Sayers's argument about the identity of Christ in your own words? Why is this argument important?
3. How helpful do you find the idea of exploring a landscape of faith?

3 Theology: five criticisms

1. How might you summarize the five objections to theology that I note in this chapter in your own words? Which seem closest to your own concerns?
2. What might someone from outside the Christian faith find valuable in theology?

3 Why do you think so many Christians are hesitant about studying theology? What reassurances could be offered to them?

4 Wisdom: discovering the depths of faith

1 Set out in your own words Karl Popper's idea of 'the three worlds'. Does this help us to think about how we can use theology?
2 What can we learn by thinking about some of the New Testament's ways of speaking about salvation?
3 How does theology help us to cope with uncertainty and doubt?

5 Wellbeing: discerning value and meaning

1 Why does meaning matter to people?
2 In what ways does theology help us to think about questions of meaning in life? You might like to focus on the doctrine of the Incarnation.
3 Why is the idea of 'the heart's desire' so important to many people? And how does theology help to identify the goal of that desire and how it might be achieved?

6 Wonder: expanding our vision of life

1 Most people think that a 'mystery' is some kind of puzzle. In what way does the theological use of the term 'mystery' differ from this?
2 What is the link between Christian worship and wonder?
3 How does the doctrine of the Trinity try to grasp the mystery of God?

7 Conclusion: making theology matter

1 Why is it important to distinguish between learning about and learning from a theologian?

2 How does John Mackay's distinction between the 'balcony' and the 'road' help us to think about how we can learn from past theologians?
3 How can we practise the art of seeing the world in a Christian way?

Notes

Introduction

1 C. S. Lewis, 'Is Theology Poetry?', in *Essay Collection & Other Short Pieces* (London: HarperCollins, 2000), pp. 10–21.

2 Julian Baggini, 'The Influential Wrongness of A. J. Ayer', *Prospect*, 12 May 2019.

1 Discovering theology: seeing things in a new way

1 Daniel Pekarsky, 'Vision and Education', in Haim Marantz ed., *Judaism and Education: Essays in Honor of Walter I. Ackerman* (Beer Sheva: Ben-Gurion University of the Negev Press, 1998).

2 Emil Brunner, 'Toward a Missionary Theology', in *Christian Century* 66, no. 27 (1949), pp. 816–18. This quote is found at p. 816.

3 Henry Miller, *Big Sur and the Oranges of Hieronymus Bosch* (New York: New Directions, 1957), p. 25.

4 Augustine, *Quaestiones in Heptateuchum*, II, 73: 'Multum et solide significatur, ad Vetus Testamentum timorem potius pertinere, sicut ad Novum dilectionem: quamquam et in Vetere Novum lateat, et in Novo Vetus pateat.'

5 For the text, see George Herbert, *The Works of George Herbert,* F. E. Hutchinson ed. (Oxford: Clarendon Press, 1945), pp. 184–5. For my own theological engagement with this fascinating poem, see Alister E. McGrath, 'The Famous Stone: The Alchemical Tropes of George Herbert's "The Elixir" in Their Late Renaissance Context', in *George Herbert Journal* 42, no. 1 & 2 (Fall 2018/Spring 2019), pp. 114–27.

6 Marilynne Robinson, *Gilead* (New York: Farrar, Straus & Giroux, 2004), p. 245.

7 Robert C. Roberts, *Spiritual Emotions: A Psychology of Christian Virtues* (Grand Rapids, MI: Eerdmans, 2007), p. 146. Italics in original.

8 See especially Alasdair C. MacIntyre, *Whose Justice? Which Rationality?* (Notre Dame, IN: University of Notre Dame Press, 1988), p. 9: 'Rationality itself, whether theoretical or practical, is a concept with a history: indeed, since there are also a diversity of traditions of enquiry, with histories, there are, so it will turn out, rationalities rather than rationality.'

9 Max Weber, *The Protestant Ethic and the Spirit of Capitalism* (London: Allen & Unwin, 1930), p. 181.

10 Letter to Edward Sackville-West, cited in Michael de-la-Noy, *Eddy: The Life of Edward Sackville-West* (London: Bodley Head, 1988), p. 237.

11 For its original statement, see C. S. Lewis, Letter to a Fifth Grade Class in Maryland, 24 May 1954; in Walter Hooper ed., *The Collected Letters of C. S. Lewis* 3 vols (San Francisco, CA: HarperOne, 2004–6), vol. 3, p. 480.

12 For my assessment of her importance, see Alister E. McGrath, 'The Owl of Minerva: Reflections on the Theological Significance of Mary Midgley', in *Heythrop Journal* 61, no. 5 (2020), pp. 852–64.

13 Charles Taylor, *Modern Social Imaginaries* (Durham, NC: Duke University Press, 2004), p. 23.

14 Charles Taylor, *Sources of the Self: The Making of the Modern Identity* (Cambridge, MA: Harvard University Press, 1989), pp. 26–31.

15 Hermann Hesse, 'Die Sehnsucht unserer Zeit nach einer Weltanschauung', in *Uhu* 2 (1926), pp. 3–14.

16 Thomas Nagel, *The Last Word* (Oxford: Oxford University Press, 1997), p. 130.
17 See Emil Brunner, 'The Other Task of Theology' (1929). For my own reflections, see Alister E. McGrath, *Emil Brunner: A Reappraisal* (Oxford: Wiley-Blackwell, 2014).
18 Alister E. McGrath, *Iustitia Dei: A History of the Christian Doctrine of Justification* 4th edn (Cambridge: Cambridge University Press, 2020), p. 413.

2 Theology as a 'big picture'

1 Eugene Wigner, 'The Unreasonable Effectiveness of Mathematics', *Communications on Pure and Applied Mathematics* 13 (1960), pp. 1–14.
2 C. S. Lewis, 'Is Theology Poetry?', in *Essay Collection & Other Short Pieces* (London: HarperCollins, 2000), pp. 12–13. *Essay Collection and Other Short Pieces* by C. S. Lewis copyright © C. S. Lewis Pte Ltd 2000. Extract reprinted by permission.
3 For this quotation and discussion of the general principles involved, see Alister McGrath, *J. I. Packer: His life and Thought* (London: Hodder & Stoughton, 2020), pp. 53–5. This image of the Bible's coherent 'Big Picture' is used by many evangelical theologians: see, for example, Vaughan Roberts, *God's Big Picture: Tracing the Storyline of the Bible* (Nottingham: Inter-Varsity Press, 2009; Downers Grove, IL: InterVarsity Press, 2002).
4 Cyril of Jerusalem, Catechesis V, 12.
5 Arie Baars, 'The Trinity', in Herman J. Selderhuis ed., *The Calvin Handbook* (Grand Rapids, MI: Eerdmans, 2009), pp. 245–57.
6 Alexander Bird, 'Scientific Realism and Three Problems for Inference to the Best Explanation', in Wenceslao J. Gonzalez

ed., *New Approaches to Scientific Realism* (Berlin: De Gruyter, 2020), pp. 48–67.

7 John Polkinghorne, *Testing Scripture: A Scientist Explores the Bible* (Grand Rapids, MI: Brazos Press, 2010), p. 1.

8 John Polkinghorne, *Science and the Trinity: The Christian Encounter with Reality* (New Haven, CT: Yale University Press, 2004).

9 For the issues, see Alister E. McGrath, *Reformation Thought: An Introduction* 5th edn (Oxford: Wiley-Blackwell, 2021), pp. 208–16.

10 C. S. Lewis, 'Meditation in a Toolshed', in C. S. Lewis, *First and Second Things* (London: Fount, 1985), p. 5. *God in the Dock* by C. S. Lewis copyright © C. S. Lewis Pte Ltd 1970. Extract reprinted by permission.

11 Karl Rahner, 'Chalkedon – Ende oder Anfang?', in Alois Grillmeier and Heinrich Bacht eds, *Das Konzil von Chalkedon: Geschichte und Gegenwart* 3 vols (Würzburg: Echter-Verlag, 1979), vol. 3, pp. 3–49.

12 For a good discussion of this, see Graham Tomlin and Nathan Eddy eds, *The Bond of Peace: Exploring Generous Orthodoxy* (London: SPCK, 2021).

13 Dorothy L. Sayers, *Creed or Chaos?* (London: Methuen, 1947), p. 28.

14 Sayers, *Creed or Chaos?*, p. 32.

15 Sayers, *Creed or Chaos?*, p. 32.

16 C. S. Lewis, *Mere Christianity* (London: HarperCollins, 2002), pp. 127–8. *Mere Christianity* by C. S. Lewis copyright © C. S. Lewis Pte Ltd 1942, 1943, 1944, 1952. Extract reprinted by permission.

17 Albert Einstein, *Ideas and Opinions* (New York: Crown Publishers, 1954), p. 38.

18 Alister E. McGrath, 'The Owl of Minerva: Reflections on the Theological Significance of Mary Midgley', in *Heythrop Journal* 61, no. 5 (2020), pp. 852–64.
19 C. S. Lewis, *Surprised by Joy* (London: HarperCollins, 2002), p. 197. *Surprised by Joy* by C. S. Lewis copyright © C. S. Lewis Pte Ltd 1955. Extract reprinted by permission.
20 Mary Midgley, *Science and Poetry* (Abingdon: Routledge, 2001), pp. 170–213.
21 For a good survey, see Brenda B. Colijn, *Images of Salvation in the New Testament* (Downers Grove, IL: IVP Academic, 2010).
22 Mary Midgley, 'Pluralism: The Many Maps Model', in *Philosophy Now* 35 (2002), pp. 10–11.

3 Theology: five criticisms

1 Alister E. McGrath, *Dawkins' God: Genes, Memes, and the Meaning of Life* (Oxford: Blackwell, 2004). A second edition of this work was published in 2015, incorporating assessment of Dawkins's later work, *The God Delusion* (London: Bantam, 2006).
2 Alister McGrath and Joanna Collicutt McGrath, *The Dawkins Delusion? Atheist Fundamentalism and the Denial of the Divine* (London: SPCK, 2007).
3 Terry Eagleton, 'Lunging, Flailing, Mispunching: A Review of Richard Dawkins' *The God Delusion*', in *London Review of Books*, 19 October 2006.
4 Richard York and Brett Clark. 2005, 'Review Essay: The Science and Humanism of Stephen Jay Gould', in *Critical Sociology* 31, nos. 1–2 (2005), pp. 281–95. See also Alister E. McGrath, 'A "Consilience of Equal Regard": Stephen Jay Gould on the Relation of Science and Religion', in *Zygon: Journal of Religion and Science* 56, no. 3 (2021), pp. 547–65.

5 Neil Postman, 'Science and the Story that We Need', in *First Things* 69 (1997), pp. 29–32.

6 Denys Turner, 'Preface', in Herbert McCabe, *Faith Within Reason* (London: Continuum, 2007), p. vii.

7 For the most influential theologians since 1990, see <https://academicinfluence.com/people?year-min=1990&discipline=theology>, accessed January 2022.

8 See Hans-Georg Gadamer, *Truth and Method* 2nd edn (London: Bloomsbury Academic, 2013), pp. 317–18.

9 For those sermons, see William H. Willemon, *The Early Preaching of Karl Barth: Fourteen Sermons* (Louisville, KY: Westminster John Knox Press, 2009).

10 The exception, of course, is his late work, *Reflections on the Psalms* (London: Geoffrey Bles, 1958), which deals with some problems that modern readers encounter in reading the text (such as its apparently harsh judgements). Lewis generally tends to engage with the Bible indirectly, through other writers.

11 John M. G. Barclay, 'Interpretation, Not Repetition: Reflections on Bultmann as a Theological Reader of Paul', *Journal of Theological Interpretation* 9, no. 2 (2015), pp. 201–9. This quote is found at p. 205.

12 Barclay, 'Interpretation, Not Repetition', p. 205. Barclay's own engagement with the Pauline letters models this approach. See John M. G. Barclay, *Paul and the Gift* (Grand Rapids, MI: Eerdmans, 2015).

13 Barclay, 'Interpretation, Not Repetition', p. 206.

14 Think, for example, of Rowan Williams's engagement with Augustine, and Sarah Coakley's retrieval of the thought of the Cappadocian writer Gregory of Nyssa (*c.*335–*c.*395). See Sarah Coakley ed., *Re-thinking Gregory of Nyssa* (Oxford: Blackwell,

2003); Rowan Williams, *On Augustine* (London: Bloomsbury, 2016).

15 For two important explorations of these points, see Edward Farley, *Theologia: The Fragmentation and Unity of Theological Education* (Philadelphia, PA: Fortress Press, 1983); Joanna Collicutt, *The Psychology of Christian Character Formation* (Norwich: SCM Press, 2015).

4 Wisdom: discovering the depths of faith

1 Karl R. Popper, 'Three Worlds', *Michigan Quarterly Review* 18, no. 1 (1979), pp. 1–23.

2 Popper, 'Three Worlds', p. 11.

3 Alfred North Whitehead, *The Aims of Education and Other Essays* (New York: Macmillan, 1929), p. 13.

4 Whitehead, *The Aims of Education*, p. 39.

5 Edward O. Wilson, *Consilience: The Unity of Human Knowledge* (New York: Alfred Knopf, 1998), p. 294.

6 Augustine, *De Catechizandis Rudibus*, ii, 3.

7 Augustine, *De Catechizandis Rudibus*, iv, 8; cf. xii, 17.

8 Carol Harrison, *The Art of Listening in the Early Church* (Oxford: Oxford University Press, 2013), p. 120.

9 Augustine, *De Catechizandis Rudibus*, v, 9.

10 Augustine of Hippo, *Sermo* LXXXVIII, v, 5.

11 Augustine, *De Catechizandis Rudibus*, xvi, 24.

12 This is a major theme in Ellen T. Charry, *By the Renewing of Your Minds: The Pastoral Function of Christian Doctrine* (Oxford: Oxford University Press, 1997).

13 Alan Jacobs, *Breaking Bread with the Dead: A Reader's Guide to a More Tranquil Mind* (New York: Penguin, 2020).

14 C. S. Lewis, *An Experiment in Criticism* (Cambridge: Cambridge University Press, 1961), pp. 140–1.

15 Rowan Williams, *On Augustine* (London: Bloomsbury, 2016) p. 132.

16 Simone Weil, *L'enracinement: Prélude à une déclaration des devoirs envers l'être humain* (Paris: Gallimard, 1949), p. 61.

17 Mary Midgley, *The Myths We Live By* (London: Routledge, 2004), p. 27.

18 These analogies are discussed in most theological textbooks. See, for example, Alister E. McGrath, *Christian Theology: An Introduction* (Oxford: Wiley-Blackwell, 2016), pp. 251–75.

19 Thomas F. Martin, 'Paul the Patient: *Christus Medicus* and the "Stimulus Carnis" (2 Cor. 12:7): A Consideration of Augustine's Medicinal Christology', *Augustinian Studies* 32, no. 2 (2001), pp. 219–56.

20 For further discussion, see Joshua Farris and S. Mark Hamilton, 'The Logic of Reparative Substitution: Contemporary Restitution Models of Atonement, Divine Justice, and Somatic Death', *Irish Theological Quarterly* 83, no. 1 (2018), pp. 62–77.

21 For further discussion, see the material in Julia Meszaros and Johannes Zachhuber eds, *Sacrifice and Modern Thought* (Oxford: Oxford University Press, 2013).

22 Miroslav Volf, 'She Who Truly Loves', *Christian Century* August 26–September 2 1998, p. 797.

23 Rebecca M. Painter, 'Further Thoughts on A Prodigal Son Who Cannot Come Home, on Loneliness and Grace: An Interview with Marilynne Robinson', *Christianity and Literature* 58, no. 3 (2009), pp. 485–92. See especially pp. 487–8.

24 For my own thoughts on this, see Alister E. McGrath, *Enriching Our Vision of Reality: Theology and the Natural Sciences in Dialogue* (London: SPCK, 2016).

25 Roy Bhaskar, *A Realist Theory of Science* (London: Verso, 2008).

26 Stephen J. Gould, *The Hedgehog, the Fox, and the Magister's Pox: Mending and Minding the Misconceived Gap between*

Science and the Humanities (London: Jonathan Cape, 2003), p. 251.

27 Graham Ward, *Unbelievable: Why We Believe and Why We Don't* (London: I. B. Tauris, 2014), pp. 127–8.

28 Bertrand Russell, *A History of Western Philosophy* (London: Allen & Unwin, 1961), p. 14.

29 Jacob Bronowski, *The Ascent of Man: A Personal View* (London: British Broadcasting Corporation, 1973), p. 353.

30 Bronowski, *The Ascent of Man*, p. 367.

31 For what follows, see John A. Mackay, *A Preface to Christian Theology* (London: Nisbet, 1941), pp. 29–54.

32 Sonnet X, 'Huntsman, What Quarry?', in Edna St. Vincent Millay, *Collected Sonnets* (New York: Harper Perennial, 1988), p. 140. Permission to reproduce sought.

33 For my reflections, see Alister E. McGrath, *Luther's Theology of the Cross: Martin Luther's Theological Breakthrough* (Oxford: Blackwell, 1985).

34 Timothy J. Wengert and Robert Kolb, *The Book of Concord: The Confessions of the Evangelical Lutheran Church* (Minneapolis, MN: Augsburg Fortress, 2000), p. 386.

35 For these quotes in their context, see Alister E. McGrath, *Luther's Theology of the Cross* (Oxford: Blackwell, 1985), pp. 148–52.

5 Wellbeing: discerning value and meaning

1 <www.vatican.va/content/benedict-xvi/en/speeches/2005/august/documents/hf_ben-xvi_spe_20050818_youth-celebration.html>, accessed January 2022. Joseph Ratzinger, widely seen as one of Germany's leading Catholic theologians, was elected Pope in April 2005, following the death of John

Paul II, and chose to be known as 'Benedict'. He retired from the papacy in 2013.

2 Miroslav Volf and Matthew Croasmun, *For the Life of the World: Theology that Makes a Difference* (Grand Rapids, MI: Brazos Press, 2019), p. 45. For a good general account of the relation of faith and wellbeing, see Andrew Briggs and Michael J. Reiss, *Human Flourishing: Scientific Insight and Spiritual Wisdom in Uncertain Times* (Oxford: Oxford University Press, 2021).

3 Ellen T. Charry, 'On Happiness', in *Anglican Theological Review* 86, no. 1 (2004), pp. 19–33. This quote is found at p. 19.

4 For my own reflections, see Alister E. McGrath, 'Christianity', in Mark Cobb, Christina Puchalski and Bruce Rumbold eds, *The Textbook of Spirituality in Healthcare* (Oxford: Oxford University Press, 2012), pp. 25–30.

5 To give an obvious example: secular humanism regards belief in God as irrational and potentially oppressive; Christianity regards belief in God as rational and liberating.

6 Charles Taylor, *The Ethics of Authenticity* (Cambridge, MA: Harvard University Press, 1991), p. 29.

7 For the problems, see the classic study of Alasdair C. MacIntyre, *Whose Justice? Which Rationality?* (Notre Dame, IN: University of Notre Dame Press, 1988).

8 Ludwig Wittgenstein, *On Certainty* (Oxford: Blackwell, 1974), p. 336.

9 Kathryn Tanner, 'Christian Claims: How My Mind Has Changed', in *Christian Century* 127, no. 4 (2010), pp. 40–5.

10 Susan R. Wolf, *The Variety of Values: Essays on Morality, Meaning, and Love* (New York: Oxford University Press, 2015), pp. 89–106. For Wolf's own engagement with this question, see

Susan R. Wolf, *Meaning in Life and Why It Matters* (Princeton, NJ: Princeton University Press, 2010).

11 Jeanette Winterson, *Why Be Happy When You Could Be Normal?* (London: Vintage, 2012), p. 68.

12 For discussion, see Genia Schönbaumsfeld, "Meaning-Dawning" in Wittgenstein's *Notebooks*', *British Journal for the History of Philosophy* 26, no. 3 (2018), pp. 540–56.

13 Michael F. Steger, 'Meaning in Life', in Shane J. Lopez ed., *Oxford Handbook of Positive Psychology* (Oxford: Oxford University Press, 2009), pp. 679–87. This quote is found at p. 682.

14 For a good account of Frankl's approach and its significance, see Paul T. P. Wong, 'Viktor Frankl's Meaning-Seeking Model and Positive Psychology', in Alexander Batthyany and Pninit Russo-Netzer eds, *Meaning in Positive and Existential Psychology* (New York: Springer, 2014), pp. 149–84.

15 Joseph Conrad, *Chance* (Oxford: Oxford University Press, 1988), p. 50.

16 William James, *The Will to Believe* (New York: Dover Publications, 1956), p. 51.

17 John Calvin, *Institutes of the Christian Religion*, III.ii,7.

18 Cited in Stephen Spencer, *Christ in All Things: William Temple and his Writings* (Norwich: Canterbury Press, 2015), p. 159.

19 Augustine, *De moribus ecclesiae catholicae*, xxv, 46. Note the obvious allusion to texts such as Mark 12.29–31.

20 Ian James Kidd, 'Adversity, Wisdom, and Exemplarism', *Journal of Value Inquiry* 52, no. 4 (2018), pp. 379–93. See also Mark Wynn, *Spiritual Traditions and the Virtues: Living between Heaven and Earth* (New York: Oxford University Press, 2020), pp. 98–133.

21 For its theological and spiritual application, see Joanna Collicutt, *The Psychology of Christian Character Formation* (Norwich: SCM Press, 2015), pp. 63–72.
22 Kathryn Tanner, *Christ the Key* (Cambridge: Cambridge University Press, 2009), p. 199.
23 Marilynne Robinson, *The Death of Adam: Essays on Modern Thought* (New York: Picador, 2005), p. 240.
24 George Herbert, *The Works of George Herbert,* F. E. Hutchinson ed. (Oxford: Clarendon Press, 1945), p. 184. For comment on this alchemical image and its significance, see Alister E. McGrath, 'The Famous Stone: The Alchemical Tropes of George Herbert's "The Elixir" in Their Late Renaissance Context', *George Herbert Journal* 42, no. 1 & 2 (Fall 2018/Spring 2019), pp. 114–27.
25 Marilynne Robinson, *Jack* (New York: Picador, 2021), p. 209.
26 David Bentley Hart, *Atheist Delusions: The Christian Revolution and Its Fashionable Enemies* (New Haven, CT: Yale University Press, 2009), p. 171.
27 Hart, *Atheist Delusions*, p. 169.
28 Hart, *Atheist Delusions*, p. 174.
29 Cited in Ilia Delio, *Simply Bonaventure: An Introduction to His Life, Thought, and Writings* (Hyde Park, NY: New City Press, 2001), p. 112.
30 Stanley Hauerwas, 'The Demands of a Truthful Story: Ethics and the Pastoral Task', *Chicago Studies* 21, no. 1 (1982), pp. 59–71. This quote is found at pp. 65–6.
31 For a fuller statement of this concern, see Gerhard Ebeling, 'Schrift und Erfahrung als Quelle theologischer Ausagen', *Zeitschrift für Theologie und Kirche* 75, no. 1 (1978), pp. 99–116.
32 Iris Murdoch, *Acastos: Two Platonic Dialogues* (Harmondsworth: Penguin, 1987), p. 61.

33 Augustine, *Confessiones*, I.i.1.
34 Rowan Williams, *On Augustine* (London: Bloomsbury, 2016), p. 208.

6 Wonder: expanding our vision of life

1 Robert C. Fuller, *Wonder: From Emotion to Spirituality* (Chapel Hill, NC: University of North Carolina Press, 2006), p. 12.
2 Michael Mayne, *This Sunrise of Wonder: Letters for the Journey* (London: Darton, Longman & Todd, 2008), p. 10.
3 Eberhard Busch, *Karl Barth: His Life from Letters and Autobiographical Texts* (Norwich: SCM Press, 1976), p. 244.
4 Henry Miller, *The Colossus of Maroussi* (London: Penguin, 2016), pp. 199–200.
5 Albert Einstein, *Ideas and Opinions* (New York: Crown Publishers, 1954), p. 38.
6 There is a large body of literature. For the article that created this interest in awe, see Dacher Keltner and Jonathan Haidt, 'Approaching Awe: A Moral, Spiritual and Aesthetic Emotion', *Cognition and Emotion* 17 (2003), pp. 297–314.
7 C. S. Lewis, *The Last Battle* (London: HarperCollins, 2011), p. 168. *The Last Battle* by C. S. Lewis copyright © C. S. Lewis Pte Ltd 1956. Extract reprinted by permission.
8 Aldous Huxley, *Brave New World Revisited* (New York: Bantam, 1960), p. 34.
9 Thomas Merton, *Life and Holiness* (New York: Image Books, 1963), p. 29.
10 Simone Weil, *Waiting for God* (New York: Putnam's Sons, 1951), p. 111.
11 Cited in Hans Urs von Balthasar, *Cosmic Liturgy: The Universe According to Maximus the Confessor* (San Francisco, CA: Ignatius Press, 2003), p. 327.

12 Bonaventure, *Breviloquium*, II.xi.2.

13 Henry Miller, *On Writing* (New York: New Directions, 1964), p. 37.

14 Denise Inge, 'A Poet Comes Home: Thomas Traherne, Theologian in a New Century', *Anglican Theological Review* 86, no. 2 (2004), pp. 335–48.

15 Thomas Traherne, *Centuries* I, 27, lines 1–5, in Denise Inge ed., *Thomas Traherne: Poetry and Prose* (London: SPCK, 2002), p. 3.

16 Michael Mayne, *This Sunrise of Wonder: Letters for the Journey* (London: Darton, Longman & Todd, 2008), p. 15. Italics as original.

17 This attentiveness to the natural world also plays into the form of discussion traditionally known as 'natural theology'. See Alister E. McGrath, *Re-Imagining Nature: The Promise of a Christian Natural Theology* (Oxford: Wiley-Blackwell, 2016).

18 Keltner and Haidt, 'Approaching Awe', pp. 305 and 310–11.

19 See Antonio Gramsci, *Gli intellettuali e l'organizzazione della cultura* 6th edn (Milan: Giulio Einaudi Editore, 1955). Sadly, at the time of writing, this has yet to be translated into English. These ideas are also set out in his prison notebooks, which were first published between 1948 and 1951.

20 For my experience, see Alister E. McGrath, *Through a Glass Darkly: Journeys through Science, Faith and Doubt* (London: Hodder & Stoughton, 2020), pp. 141–50.

21 Antonio Gramsci, *Quaderni del carcere* 4 vols (Turin: Giulio Einaudi Editore, 1975), vol. 1, p. 56.

22 For these citations and a fuller analysis, see John Heeren, 'Karl Mannheim and the Intellectual Elite', *British Journal of Sociology* 22, no. 1 (1971), pp. 1–15.

23 Cited in Helen Dukas and Banesh Hoffman eds, *Albert Einstein, the Human Side: New Glimpses from His*

Archives (Princeton, NJ: Princeton University Press, 1979), p. 39.

24 Letter to A. Chapple, Australia, February 23 1954; Einstein Archive 59–405.

25 Werner Heisenberg, *Die Ordnung der Wirklichkeit* (Munich: Piper Verlag, 1989), pp. 38–52. This quote is found at p. 44.

26 Thomas G. Weinandy, *Does God Suffer?* (Notre Dame, IN: University of Notre Dame Press, 2000), p. 32.

27 Hilary of Poitiers, *De Trinitate*, II, 2.

28 For Reginald's account, see Marjorie O'Rourke Boyle, 'Chaff: Thomas Aquinas's Repudiation of his *Opera Omnia*', *New Literary History* 28, no. 2 (1997), pp. 383–99. Many accounts of this incident incorrectly translate the Latin word *palea* as 'straw'.

29 Tomáš Halík, 'Church for the Seekers', in Tomáš Halík and Pavel Hošek eds, *A Czech Perspective on Faith in a Secular Age* (Washington, DC: Council for Research in Values and Philosophy, 2015), pp. 127–33. This quote is found at p. 128.

30 Thomáš Halík, *Night of the Confessor: Christian Faith in an Age of Uncertainty* (New York: Doubleday, 2012), p. 59.

31 Tomáš Halík, *Patience with God: The Story of Zacchaeus Continuing in Us* (New York: Doubleday, 2009), p. ix.

32 Halík, *Patience with God*, p. 46.

33 Hilary of Poitiers, *De Trinitate*, II.5.

34 See George Hunsinger, 'Karl Barth's Doctrine of the Trinity, and Some Protestant Doctrines after Barth', in Giles Emery and Matthew Levering eds, *The Oxford Handbook of the Trinity* (Oxford: Oxford University Press, 2012), pp. 294–313.

35 Emil Brunner, *Der Mittler: Zur Besinnung über den Christusglauben* 4th edn (Zurich: Zwingli-Verlag, 1947), pp.

243–4. For my own reflections on Brunner's approach to the Trinity, see Alister E. McGrath, *Emil Brunner: A Reappraisal* (Oxford: Wiley-Blackwell, 2014), pp. 50–4 and 234–7.

36 Catherine Mowry LaCugna, *God for Us: The Trinity and the Christian Life* (San Francisco, CA: HarperSanFrancisco, 1973), p. 1.

37 Catherine Mowry LaCugna, 'The Practical Trinity', *Christian Century* 109, no. 22 (1992), pp. 678–82. This quote is found at p. 682.

38 Augustine, *De Trinitate*, I.viii.18.

39 For this concern, see G. E. R. Lloyd, *Disciplines in the Making: Cross-Cultural Perspectives on Elites, Learning, and Innovation* (Oxford: Oxford University Press, 2009).

40 For an influential criticism of this development, see Edward Farley, *Theologia: The Fragmentation and Unity of Theological Education* (Philadelphia, PA: Fortress Press, 1983).

41 Good examples are the bestselling evangelical writers J. I. Packer (who draws extensively on the English Puritan writer John Owen) and John Piper (who develops the ideas of the American Puritan writer Jonathan Edwards).

42 Ellen T. Charry, *By the Renewing of Your Minds: The Pastoral Function of Christian Doctrine* (Oxford: Oxford University Press, 1997), p. 236.

43 Pierre Hadot, *Études de philosophie antique* (Paris: Les Belles Lettres, 2010), pp. 207–32.

44 Sarah Coakley, *Powers and Submissions: Spirituality, Philosophy, and Gender* (Oxford: Blackwell, 2002) p. 34.

45 J. I. Packer, 'An Introduction to Systematic Spirituality', *Crux* 26, no. 1 (1990), pp. 2–8.

46 C. S. Lewis, 'Is Theology Poetry?', in *Essay Collection & Other Short Pieces* (London: HarperCollins, 2000), pp. 10–21. *Essay*

Collection and Other Short Pieces by C. S. Lewis copyright © C. S. Lewis Pte Ltd 2000. Extract reprinted by permission.

7 Conclusion: making theology matter

1 Sohrab Ahmari, *The Unbroken Thread: Discovering the Wisdom of Tradition in an Age of Chaos* (London: Hodder & Stoughton, 2021).
2 William James, *The Varieties of Religious Experience: A Study in Human Nature* (London: Longmans, Green & Co., 1911), p. 151.
3 There is a large body of literature. Some useful gateways can be found in Rowan Williams's *Being Christian: Baptism, Bible, Eucharist, Prayer* (London: SPCK, 2014); Joanna Collicutt, *The Psychology of Christian Character Formation* (Norwich: SCM Press, 2015); Michael J. Gorman, *Participating in Christ: Explorations in Paul's Theology and Spirituality* (Grand Rapids, MI: Baker Academic, 2019).
4 James K. A. Smith, *On the Road with Saint Augustine* (Grand Rapids, MI: Brazos, 2019).
5 For a good example of an accessible work that aims to do this, see Rowan Williams's *Luminaries: Twenty Lives that Illuminate the Christian Way* (London: SPCK, 2020).
6 Readers wanting to study these should turn to Benedicta Ward's admirable translation of these writings in the 'Penguin Classics' series. See *The Prayers and Meditations of Saint Anselm with the Proslogion* (Harmondsworth: Penguin, 1973).
7 See, for example, the caustic comments of John Gray, *Seven Types of Atheism* (London: Penguin, 2018), pp. 9–23.